C000173538

The Templar's Curse

The Templar's Curse

Evelyn Lord

PEARSON

Longman

Harlow, England • London • New York • Boston • San Francisco • Toronto
Sydney • Tokyo • Singapore • Hong Kong • Seoul • Taipei • New Delhi
Cape Town • Madrid • Mexico City • Amsterdam • Munich • Paris • Milan

PEARSON EDUCATION LIMITED

Edinburgh Gate
Harlow CM20 2JE
United Kingdom
Tel: +44 (0)1279 623623
Fax: +44 (0)1279 431059
Website: www.pearsoned.co.uk

First edition published in Great Britain in 2008

ISBN: 978-1-4058-4038-5

British Library Cataloguing in Publication Data
Lord, Evelyn.
    The Templar's curse / Evelyn Lord.
        p.   cm.
    Includes bibliographical references and index.
    ISBN 978-1-4058-4038-5 (hardback)
1. Templars–History.   2. Templars–France–Trials, litigation, etc.
3. Trials (Heresy)–Europe–History.   I. Title.
CR4749.L67 2007
271'.79–dc22

                                        2007042093

A CI_____ for this book can be obtained from the British Library

10   9   8   7   6   5   4   3   2   1
11   10   09   08   07

Typeset by 35 in 9.5/14pt Melior
Printed and bound by Henry Ling Ltd, Dorchester, Dorset

The Publisher's policy is to use paper manufactured from sustainable forests.

To my family past and present, with love

Contents

List of illustrations

List of maps

Grand Masters of the Knights Templar

Hugh de Payens	1118–36
Robert de Craon	1136–49
Everard des Barres	1149–52
Bernard de Tremblay	1153
Andrea de Montbord	1154–6
Bertrard de Blanchefort	1156–69
Philip de Nablus (or de Milly)	1169–71
Odo de St Armand	c.1171–9
Arnald de Torroja	1181–4
Gerard de Ridefort	1185–9
Robert de Sablé	1191–3
Gilbert Erail	1194–1200
Philip de Plessis	1201–9
William de Chartres	1210–19
Peter de Montaigne	1219–32
Armand de Perigord	c.1232–45
William de Sonnac	c.1245–50
Reginald de Vichiers	1250–6
Thomas Berard	1256–73
William de Beaujeu	1273–91
Theobald Gaudin	1291–3
Jacques de Molay	1293–1314

Sources: M. Barber, *The New Knighthood*, Cambridge: CUP, p. xxiii the international website of the Order of Templars, at: www.ordotempli. org/grand_masters_of_our_order.htm; some names have been given in a different form from this source.

A Crusade and Templar chronology

1188 Templar's castle at Baghras captured

1189 Third Crusade

1191 Templars buy Cyprus but sell it the next year

1192 Crusaders at Ascalon
      Truce with Saladin

1193 Death of Saladin

1204 Fourth Crusade: Constantinople taken by the crusaders and sacked

1211 Templars make a raid on Damietta from the sea

1218 Fifth Crusade

1219 St Francis of Assisi preaches to the crusaders
      The crusaders take Damietta

1228 Frederick II's crusade

1229 Frederick takes Jerusalem in March, returns to Italy in May

1240 Mongol threat to the western states

1241 Templars and Hospitallers fall out. The Templars besiege the
      Hospitallers' house at Acre
      The Templars' raid into Hebron, followed by a retaliation attack
      on pilgrims

1242 Templars sack Nablus. Retaliation by Egypt

1244 Battle of La Forbie: Christians defeated
      Ascalon and Jaffa fall to the Muslims

1248 Louis IX's crusade

1249 Crusaders occupy Damietta

1250 Battle of Mansurah, Louis IX captured and ransomed

1258 Mongols destroy Baghdad

1259 Mongols invade Syria, Poland and Lithuania

1260 Mongols capture Damascus

1264 Templars and Hospitallers attack Ascalon. Retaliation against
      Caeserea and the Templar Castle Pilgrim

1266 The Templar castle of Safet falls to Baybars

1267 Louis IX's second crusade

1271 The Templar Castle Blanc surrenders to Baybars. The Templars
      withdraw to Tortosa

1291 Siege and capture of Acre: Templars withdraw to Cyprus

1292 Jacques de Molay elected Grand Master

1306 Jacques de Molay asked by the pope to consider the unification of
      the Templars and Hospitallers. Leaves Cyprus for France

1307	14 September:	Philip IV issues secret orders for the arrests of the Templars
	13 October:	All French Templars arrested
	19 October:	Hearings against the Templars begin
	24 October:	Jacques de Molay's confession
1308	February:	Clement V suspends the inquisition against the Templars
	May:	Philip IV arrives at Poitiers to see Clement
	June:	72 selected Templars sent by Philip to Clement
1309	Spring:	Papal commission of inquiry into the Templars opens
	November:	Jacques de Molay appears before the commission
1310	March:	Mass meeting of the Templars to prepare a defence of the Order
	April:	Attempts made to defend the Order
	May:	70 Templars burnt at the stake
1311	June:	Papal commission ends
	October:	Opening of the Council of Vienne
1312	May:	Suppression of the Order of the Knights Templar
1314	March:	Jacques de Molay burnt at the stake

Templars and Britain chronology

1086   Domesday Book

1087   Death of William I. Accession of William II, his second son

1100   Death of William II. Accession of Henry I, his brother

1120   White Ship disaster: drowning of Henry's heir

1128   The Knights Templar come to Britain

1135   Death of Henry I. Accession of Stephen, his nephew
Templars at the Old Temple in London

1139   Matilda Henry's daughter, claims the throne. Civil war.

1140   The Anarchy. Battle of Lincoln

1144   Death of Geoffrey de Mandeville, Matilda's supporter at the siege of Burwell. His body taken by the Templars to the Old Temple

1154   Death of Stephen. Accession of Matilda's son Henry II

1161   Templars move to the New Temple

1170   Murder of Thomas à Becket on Henry's orders

1185   The Great Inquest of the Templars' lands in England taken

1189   Death of Henry II. Accession of Richard I his son

1192   Imprisonment of Richard by the Duke of Austria on his way home from the Third Crusade

1199   Death of Richard I. Accession of John his brother

1209   Excommunication of John and the whole of England

1213   John pays homage to the pope following an agreement brokered at the Templars' house at Dover

1214   John buys a second-hand ship from the Templars

1215   Magna Carta. John spent the night before Runnymede at the New Temple

1216   Death of John. Accession of Henry III his son

1232   Fall of Hubert de Burgh, whose treasure was in the New Temple

1245   Henry III's treasure deposited at the New Temple

1250   Henry takes the Cross, but eventually commutes this vow to a fine, rather than go to the Holy Land

1264   Henry at war with his barons led by Simon de Montfort
       Battle of Lewes. Henry defeated

1265   Battle of Evesham. Simon de Montfort defeated and killed

1270   The Lord Edward (future Edward I) on crusade

1271   Death of Henry III. Accession of Edward I, his son

1274   Edward returns to England from his crusade

1277   Edward starts building castles in Wales to consolidate his conquests there

1284   Birth of Edward II at Caernarvon Castle; dubbed Prince of Wales

1290   Expulsion of the Jews from England

1294   Edward's conquest of Wales complete

1295   War with Scotland

1298   William de la More, the last Templar master of England, chosen

1299   Parliament held at the New Temple

1307   Edward I dies on his way to Scotland. Accession of Edward II his son

30 October:	Edward II's expresses his incredulity about the Templars' arrest in France and their guilt
November:	Papal bull against the Templars
4 December:	Edward sends letters to other European princes defending the: Templars
10 December:	Edward writes to the pope that he believes in the Templars' innocence
14 December:	Edward receives the papal bull authorising the arrest of the Templars
15 December:	Edward's order to the county sheriffs telling them to muster 24 men to attend to hear a mandate from the king to arrest the Templars
26 December:	Edward writes to the pope to tell him what he has done
30 December:	Sealed mandates sent to the sheriffs

1308   9–10 January: English Templars arrested
       February: Edward II marries Isabella of France

1309   20 October–18 November first process against the English Templars in London

	November:	Trial of the Scottish Templars
	13 December:	Hostile witnesses heard in London. Trial of the Scottish Templars
1310	January:	Trial of the Irish Templars
	February:	Trial resumes in London
	March:	Pressure put on Edward II to obtain confessions by torture
		Templars in Lincoln Castle examined
	April:	Templars in the Tower of London chained and placed in solitary confinement
		Trial of Templars in York Castle
	May:	Edward tells the sheriffs of York and Lincoln to treat the Templars and their bodies according to ecclesiastical law
	August:	Constable of the Tower of London told to put the Templars into the keeping of the Sheriff of London
1311	March:	Templars in Lincoln Castle taken to London
	April:	William de la More publicly proclaims the Templars' innocence
	June:	Confessions of guilt by three apostate Templars
	July–August:	Public confessions of guilt of other Templars except William de la More and Himbert Blank
		William de la More sent to the Tower of London where he died. The other Templars sent to monasteries to do penance
1324		Deeds and charters of Templar lands handed over to the Knights Hospitaller

Preface

The year 2007 marked the 700th anniversary of the arrest of the Knights Templar. Once they were a renowned band of crusading knights, but in 1307 they were accused of corruption, heresy, idolatry and sodomy. Their guilt and the fate of their fabled treasure and the secrets they were alleged to hold have intrigued authors, historians, theologians and treasure-seekers over the centuries, whilst the immense success of Dan Brown's novel *The Da Vinci Code* has brought the Templars and their secrets before the public as never before. Now thousands flock to the sites mentioned in Brown's book, looking for the codes, and hoping to solve the mystery for themselves. But were the Knights Templar the holders of secrets that could destroy the faith of the western world, or an organisation of knights simply fighting for what they believed in? Their success in attracting gifts of property and riches to their order also created jealousy and led to accusations of corruption which accumulated over time, and led at last to their downfall at the hands of a determined king of France and a weak pope.

However, the glamour of the knight of the red cross setting out on a quest remains with us, and we all love a mystery. The Knights Templar, the clash of swords on armour down the ages, and a dedication to a cause which they thought was right will stay within Western culture for many hundreds of years to come, whilst the 700th anniversary of their descent into imprisonment and death is an appropriate time to celebrate them.

Acknowledgements

Thanks to the staff of Cambridge University Library, Colleagues at the Institute of Continuing Education, my students – past and present, Professor Jonathan Riley-Smith, the editorial team at Pearson Education, Mr Phillip Judge who drew the maps and the realization of the Paris Temple, Mr Duncan McAra, and last but not least Gabriel and Edward Lord.

Publisher's acknowledgements

W̶e are grateful to the following for permission to reproduce copyright material:

Plate 1, The Masters and Fellows of Corpus Christi College Cambridge; Plate 2, © British Library Board. All Rights Reserved (Royal 16 G. VI); Plate 3, Visual Arts Library (London)/Alamy; Plate 4, © Bibliotheque Nationale, Paris, France/Giraudon/The Bridgeman Art Library; Plate 5, © British Library, London, UK/The Bridgeman Art Library; Plate 6, Phillip Judge; Plate 7, Mark Lucas/Alamy; Plate 8, © British Library Board. All Rights Reserved (Royal 20 C. VII); Maps 1–3, Phillip Judge.

In some instances we have been unable to trace the owners of copyright material and we would appreciate any information that would enable us to do so.

Prologue

Paris, 18 March 1314

An island in the Seine. Two men dressed only in their shirts stand beside a pyre. One is Jacques de Molay, Grand Master of the Knights Templar. The other is Geoffroi de Charney, preceptor of the Knights Templar in Normandy. Their hands are tied. Jostled and pushed, they are bound to the stake. Flaming brands wait to set the pyre alight. Jacques de Molay speaks:

> *'Gentlemen,*
> *At least untie my hands a moment*
> *So I may make my orison to God.*
> *I vow it is the time and season of my death,*
> *I see here my judgement,*
> *But death pleases me.*
> *God knows who is in the wrong and who has sinned.*
> *In a brief time he will gather them in,*
> *Those who have wrongly condemned us.*
> *God will revenge our death.'*
> *'Gentlemen,' he said, 'Know that throughout the land*
> *All who are against us*
> *Will suffer for us.*
> *This is my faith.*
> *At this time, I beg you*
> *That I may see the Virgin Mary.*
> *Turn my face to her*
> *That I may see her as I die.'*[1]

Geoffroi de Paris reports:

This request was granted
And so gently did death take him
That everyone marvelled.[2]

A month later on 20 April 1314 Pope Clement V, who had helped to condemn the Knight Templar, died. The chief persecutor of the Knights Templar, Philip IV of France, followed him to the grave on 29 November 1314. It seemed God was avenging de Molay's death, just as he had foretold; and famine, plague and revolt were to follow as the Templar's curse came home to roost.

How did Jacques de Molay come to stand before the stake? Why had the Knights Templar, previously known as a noble band of Crusaders and protectors of pilgrims to the Holy Land, come to this sorry situation? Were they the innocent victims of an avaricious king and a cowardly pope? What happened to the members of the Order who survived the trials, the burnings and the Order's suppression? These are questions this book will answer.

I will start by describing the foundation of the Order, and its exploits in the Holy Land, before moving on to the crucial events of 1307–14 when a tangled web of politics, religion, greed and intrigue led Jacques de Molay to the pyre and resulted in the suppression of the Order. Finally I will discuss the legends of the Knights Templar and how these have evolved over time. This is a book designed for the general reader interested in history and the Knights Templar to enjoy, but it includes a detailed bibliography so that areas of especial interest to a reader can be followed up in more detail. It aims to set the Templars and the crusades with which they were involved in context but without losing sight of either their grisly end, or the disbanding of an Order which still exerts a pull on the imagination today.

Notes

1 *La Chronique métrique attribuée à Geofroi de Paris*, ed. A. Diverrès, trans. E. Lord, Strasbourg: Faculty of Letters of the University of Strasbourg, (1957), p. 199.

2 Ibid.

CHAPTER 1

· · · · · · · · · · · · · ·

The foundation of the Order

In 1099 the First Crusade took Jerusalem for the Christians. This unleashed a flood of pilgrims hastening to the Holy City and the places described in the New Testament in order to gain redemption from their sins. These innocent and unprepared travellers became a prey for robbers, Saracens and wild animals. They died in their hundreds as they tried to retrace the steps of Christ from Jerusalem to the River Jordan, the desert and the Sea of Galilee.

In Jerusalem at this time were a group of French knights, led by Hugh de Payens. They may have been part of the First Crusade, or have come to the Holy Land as pilgrims themselves. How or why they were in Jerusalem is not known. Nor is the date when they founded their order of monkish knights. Was it as a response to the slaughter of 300 pilgrims at Easter 1119? Or was it earlier than this? William, Archbishop of Tyre, writing after the event, suggests that the Order was founded in 1118 when 'certain pious and God-fearing nobles of knightly rank devoted to the Lord, professed the wish to live perpetually in poverty, chastity and obedience. In the hands of the Patriarch they vowed themselves to the service of God as regular canons.' At this point they had taken religious vows, but as yet were not a military order. Tyre continues.

> Foremost and most distinguished among these men were the venerable
> Hugh de Payens and Godfrey de St Omer. Since they had neither church,
> nor a fixed place of abode the king granted them a temporary dwelling
> place in his own palace, on the north side of the Temple of the Lord . . .
> The main duty of this order – that which was enjoined upon them by the

patriarch and other bishops for the remission of sins – was that, as far as
their strength was permitted they should keep the roads and highways
safe from the menace of robbers and highwaymen, with especial regard
for the protection of pilgrims . . . 'Nine years after the founding of the
order the knights were still in secular garb. They wore such garments as
the people, for the salvation of their souls bestowed upon them. During
the ninth year a council was held at Troyes. . . .'[1]

The story of the Order's foundation was embroidered by Walter Map, who was a clerk in the household of Henry II, king of England in the 1170s. He attributed the foundation of the Order entirely to the bravery of Hugh de Payens who single-handedly fought off the Saracens who attacked pilgrims that came to drink at the Red Pool. Word of de Payens's deeds came to the regular canons of Jerusalem who gave him a large hall in the Temple of Solomon, where he was joined by his knightly companions.[2]

Hugh de Payens and the Temple of Solomon

Like so many aspects of the Knights Templar much of the detail surrounding their foundation is shrouded in mystery. We know that it was founded by Hugh de Payens, who became the Order's first Grand Master. Hugh de Payens may have come from a village of that name in Champagne, and his overlord the Count of Champagne may have played an important part in the subsequent course of the Order, as he was an intimate of St Bernard of Clairvaux, the Templars' patron.

The original members of the Order (see Box 1.1) were knights who took monastic vows of poverty, chastity and obedience. According to a thirteenth-century chronicler, Matthew Paris, this was to gain remission from their sins.[3] They were known collectively as 'brothers' and when not in the saddle they lived a cloistered life dedicated to the worship of God.

The Order's first dwelling place was in the Temple of Solomon and there is proof of this not only from tradition, but also from the evidence of a German monk Theoderic, who visited Jerusalem in 1174 and left a description of the knights' precinct in the Temple of Solomon. They may have been given these premises by King Baldwin of Jerusalem as William of Tyre suggested, or by the patriarch of Jerusalem or the canons of the Holy Sepulchre.

Box 1.1 Founder knights of the Knights templar

Hugh de Payens, First Grand Master
Andrea de Montbord
Archimbaud de St Armand from Picardy
Geoffroy Bisol or Bisot
Godfrey de St Omer from Picardy
Payen de Montdidier from Picardy
Roland or Rossol

Although the Order's original aim was to protect pilgrims, this was a body of knights trained in arms and warfare and possessing a great deal of aggressive energy. If this could be harnessed into fighting for God and the Christian occupation of the Holy Land, they believed they would gain absolution for their sins through the practical application of the life they knew best – combat – and would be doing the whole of Christendom an inestimable service.

It soon became clear that a handful of knights would not succeed in stemming the flow of the enemies of Christ into the Holy Land. Men, money and resources were needed. In order to acquire these, the western powers had to be wooed into recognizing the Order and sponsoring it by granting it resources. In 1127 Hugh and five companions left the East for the Council of Troyes in France to put the case for the Order, and to establish it firmly in western minds by promoting the idea that a man dedicated by his vows to the service of God could spill blood – provided it was not Christian blood.

Hugh put his case to the Council of Troyes on 13 January 1129. He already had an advocate at the council, St Bernard of Clairvaux, who had been alerted to Hugh's presence at the council by the Count of Champagne. Bernard was the energetic and articulate young nobleman who became abbot of Clairvaux, daughter house of Citeaux, the first monastery of the reforming Cistercian order. Bernard and Hugh came from the same background and understood each other.

It was Bernard who had given the Cistercians their identity as a separate order, and had drawn up the strict guidelines by which they were to live. He now did the same for the Knights Templar, and the Templar Rule had many similarities to the Cistercian Statutes, though making allowances for times when the Knights Templar were out of the cloister and on campaign. It is possible that St Bernard saw the Templars as an instrument for bringing the whole of the Holy Land under Christian control, and J.T. Fowler claims that he may have seen the Templars as the military wing of the Cistercians, although there is no evidence for this.[5]

The Templar Rule

The Rule drawn up at the Council of Troyes for the Templars starts by describing how Hugh came to the Council and told them about his order of monkish knights. Those who heard him are listed, and the preamble states that the rules were approved by the pope and the patriarch of Jerusalem. The rules go into every detail of the Order's life. They describe who could join the Order: this was limited to freemen and adult males; no serfs or women were allowed to join the Templars, but married men could enrol provided that their wives were either dead or in a nunnery, or they could become associate members for a specific time. From the start the Order was designed for the elite members of society, and was to be a totally male institution.

The Rule describes how the reception of those joining the Order should take place. At the reception the initiate was to declare that he was a freeman in good health, and had no outstanding debts. He asked to be a knight of Christ in holy orders and would renounce his own free will. Once he had been accepted by those present the Templar Rule was explained to him and he knelt with both hands on the Gospels and promised his life to God and the Blessed Virgin. He vowed to be chaste, to live a life of poverty and to be obedient to God and the Order. The Templar mantle was placed around his neck, and the chaplain and whoever was conducting the reception would raise him up and kiss him on the mouth. This reception format was open to misinterpretation, and it became one of the chief planks in the case against the Templars.

The Rule showed how life in the cloister and on campaign was to be governed. In the cloister the Templars were to live a monastic life, attending the daily offices and observing absolute silence. Discipline in the cloister was to be maintained through chapter meetings where brothers could either confess their errors, or be accused by others. They were then punished and absolved. This too became open to misinterpretation.

Brothers could be expelled from the Order for revealing its secrets, for simony (buying preferment), for killing a Christian, for theft, for desertion in the time of battle, for desertion to the enemy, and for sodomy. Lesser crimes – for which the brother lost the Templar habit for a time, was put in irons and treated like a dog, including being made to eat his food of the floor – included disobedience, striking another brother, contact with a woman, and charging into battle without permission. These statutes were to have repercussions later as well. When on campaign the Templars had to say paternosters whilst in the saddle.

The Hierarchical Statutes that were added to the rule in 1165 when the Order had become fully operational show that the structure of the Order mirrored that of feudal society (see chapter 4). It was divided into:

Knights, from the landholding class. Knights wore a white mantle and were allocated four horses;

Squires: Each knight was allowed a squire. He wore a black or brown mantle and was allocated one horse;

Sergeants: freemen, either craftsmen or farmers. They wore a brown mantle and were allocated one horse;

Servants: lay people who received board and lodgings at the order's preceptories in return for service;

Chaplains: the Order's priests.

The High Officers in the order were:

The Grand Master: overall commander of the Order;

The Seneschal: the Grand Master's deputy who took over if the Grand Master was killed in;

The Marshal: head of the military side of the Order's affairs;

The Treasurer: officer in charge of the Order's finances;

The Draper: officer in charge of providing clothes and bed linen;

The Standard Bearer: responsible for carrying the black-and-white banner into battle;

Provincial Masters and Commanders: officers in command of the Order's provinces, for example England, Scotland or Aragon;

Visitors: inspectors appointed by the Grand Master to visit and inspect each province.

When fighting in the Holy Land the Templars employed as Mercenaries lightly mounted turcopoliers who were accustomed to desert fighting. They also used Arab interpreters. Later these features of their strategy would be seen as 'consorting with the enemy'.

The Council of Troyes made the pope the overall commander of the Order, and it was to him and him alone that the Templars owed allegiance. This turned out to be a dangerous provision as it meant that the Templars had no loyalty to secular princes either in the East or the West. The Order was also given special privileges by successive popes. These included freedom from paying tithes and other ecclesiastical taxes, and the right to have their own priests who could celebrate mass and give absolution. They could have their own consecrated graveyards and could bury any one they wished in these. They were promised financial support from papal taxes, and given permission to build towns and churches in desert places. When a country was under an interdict that excommunicated all citizens the Templars were allowed to open their churches once a year to celebrate mass for the local population and to give absolution.

These privileges made the Order unpopular with other religious foundations, and with the population at large who struggled to pay tithes and taxes. William of Tyre accused the Templars of having possessions that were the equal of kings, of carrying off plunder from the Holy Land, and of a lack of humility.[6] Although the arrests in 1307 came as a shock to the Templars and a surprise to the general population the Order was not without its critics from its foundation onwards.

De laude novae militae: in praise of the new knighthood

One criticism levelled at the Order was inescapable, given their role of knights as well as monks – that they were responsible for the spilling of blood. The clamour against this seems to have hampered recruitment. In desperation Hugh de Payens asked Bernard of Clairvaux for help. The result was a tract *De laude novae militae* or 'In Praise of the New Knighthood'. In this St Bernard created the image of a perfect knight triumphing over evil and the infidel. In fighting evil the Templars were justified in spilling blood, and those brothers who died in the cause were accounted martyrs whose souls would go straight to heaven.

There is a prologue and five chapters in *De laude novae militae*. The prologue starts with an apology from St Bernard for taking so long to write the tract, as he had been asked many times by Hugh de Payens to write an exhortation for him and his comrades. Chapter 1 continues the theme of the exhortation. It promotes the Knights Templar as a new kind of knighthood waging war against the flesh and the spiritual army of evil. Chapter 2 compares the spiritual knighthood of the Templars with worldly knights who fight with pomp and cover their horses with silk, their armour with plumes, paint their shields and saddles, adorn their spurs with gold and silver and precious stones. Such knights have insecure consciences, says St Bernard: Chapter 3 portrays the Knights of Christ as safe in fighting battles for the Lord. They may strike with confidence and die knowing they serve Christ. In Chapter 4 it is suggested that the lifestyle of the Knights of the Temple should become a model for other knights, while Chapter 5 describes the Temple of Solomon where they dwelt.[7]

St Bernard's public-relations job worked and by the time Hugh de Payens died in about 1136 the Order was well established and had estates and property in the West as well as in the East. Part of Hugh's mission to the West had been to seek grants of land and rents to provide revenues for the struggle in the East. Spurred on by the pope and St Bernard secular lords gave generously to the Order, which was to become a significant landlords in Britain, France, Iberia, Italy and elsewhere in Europe. As the Templars' European estates grew in size so these were divided into linguistic provinces, each with its own master, but subservient to the Grand Master. Commanderies were established to run the estates and the Knight Templar became a recognized figure in the local landscape, distinguished by the white mantle and robe of the knights with its eight-pointed red cross, and the black or brown mantles of the sergeants.

The Templar Rule instructed brothers to keep their hair short, but not to shave. One of the features noted at the trial of the Templars was that some of the witnesses had shaved off their beards. The rule described the black-and-white Templar pennant, which was divided horizontally with the white at the bottom. This may represent the two classes of fighting men in the Order, the sergeants and the knights, or it may represent the triumph of good over evil. The Piebald Banner was an important symbol for the Templars, and a rallying point in battle that should not be allowed to fall.

Equipped with papal approval and a Rule by which to live, Hugh de Payens and his band returned East to continue their struggle there.

Notes

1   William of Tyre (1948), *A History of Deeds Done Beyond the Sea*, trans. E. Babcock and A.C. Krey, New York: Columbia University Press, Vol.1: 524–5.

2   Map, W. (1923) *De Nugis Curialium*, ed. F.S. Hartland and M.R. James, Cymmrodian Record Series, ix, 29.

3   Paris, M. (1883) *Chronica Majora* ed. Luard, H. HMSO, Rolls series 57.

4   Wilkinson, J. with J. Hill and W. Ryan (eds) (1988) *Jerusalem Pilgrimages 1099–1185*, The Hakluyt Society, 2nd series, Vol. 167.

5   Fowler, J.T. (1890), *Cistercian Statutes AD 1256–7*, Bradbury & Co., 5.

6   Tyre, 526–7.

7   Clairvaux, Bernard (1977), *In Praise of the New Knighthood*, trans. Conrad Greenia, Cistercian Fathers Series, Cistercian Publications, 127–45.

CHAPTER 2

Crusade

Why were the Crusades necessary?

The crusades in which the Knights Templar were involved were the result of the rise of Islam, which following the death of its founder, the Prophet Mohammad in AD 632 quickly spread across the East and by conquest into Europe, to become one of the world's greatest religions. At first Christians, Muslims and Jews coexisted peacefully, but by the eleventh century the Christians were also expanding their territory and seeking to re-take those parts of Europe in Muslim hands – parts of what is now Spain and Sicily.

More important than this to the Christian was Jerusalem with its iconic meaning in the life of Christ. Jerusalem was the ultimate destination of Christian pilgrims, but Jerusalem was also a holy site for the Muslims as it was where Mohammad was believed to have ascended to heaven. The city was equally holy to the Jews as it was the site of the Temple of Solomon and other sites sacred to Judaism. An Arab visitor to the city in 1047 was well aware of the city's importance to all three religions:

> By 5th March 1047 I was in Jerusalem. The people of Syria call Jerusalem the Holy City. Anyone of that province who cannot perform the pilgrimage to Mecca will visit Jerusalem, and there perform the statutory rites and offer a sacrifice . . . From Byzantine and other regions come Christians and Jews in large numbers to worship at their churches and synagogues . . .[1]

The Dome of the Rock, a mosque built in AD 700 is the Muslim's most holy place in Jerusalem; the Church of the Holy Sepulchre is the Christians' holiest site; and the Western Wall held to be the last remaining part of the Temple, is special to the Jews.

> *Jerusalem is the navel of the world, a land which is fruitful above all others, like another paradise of delights. The redeemer of the human race illuminated this land by his coming, graced it by his living there, made it holy by his suffering, redeemed it by his death, distinguished it by his burial. This royal city set in the centre of the world, is now held captive by its enemies and is enslaved by heathen rite by people who do not know God. Therefore the city demands and desires to be set free, and calls upon you without ceasing to come to its assistance . . . Therefore take this journey for the remission of your sins, certain of the unfading glory of the kingdom of heaven.*[2]

Jerusalem was the prize for three religions, but by the tenth century it was in the hands of Islam. The city had been captured from the Byzantine Christian empire by the Arabs in AD 638 and had remained in their hands. Despite this Christians still visited Jerusalem on pilgrimages, and Christians and Jews already living in Palestine were allowed freedom to worship as they wished.

By the tenth century, Byzantium, the traditional protector of Christian pilgrims to the Holy Land, was under threat from the Turks, a nomadic people from the Eurasian steppes who had converted to Islam. They were described by Christian writers as death-dealing dragons, striking against Christianity. Under extreme pressure the Byzantine emperor Alexius I Commenus (1081–1118) sent an envoy to Pope Urban II asking for help. The pope responded by preaching a sermon that asked all Christian men to join an expedition to help the emperor.[3] The idea of liberating Jerusalem was seized upon by those who heard him speak, and this became the expedition's main objective.

The Christian armies agreed to muster near to Constantinople, and eventually men at arms from all over Europe gathered together in what is now Turkey in June 1097. The response had been enormous. It is estimated that about 60,000 men enlisted, and this included 7,000 knights.[4] Although most European Catholic countries were represented, all the leaders were either French or Norman.

From Anatolia (Turkey) the army besieged and took Nicae for the Christians, and then moved inexorably forward. Antioch was taken in June 1098, and from there the way to Jerusalem lay open. The Christian army arrived outside Jerusalem on 7 June 1099.[5] The city surrendered on 15 July and the Christians entered Jerusalem as conquerors. It is probable that the founder members of the Knights Templar were part of this army and remained in the city after the other Christians had returned home. The expedition, which we now know as the First Crusade, had achieved its objective.

What Was a Crusade

The word *crusade* comes from the Latin word for the cross, *crux*, although Peter Lock argues that the term 'crusade' was never used in the middle ages. The Knights Templar and their contemporaries referred to the expeditions against the Muslims as 'taking the cross', and this is how it was described by Gerald of Wales,[6] who was part of a mission to persuade men to enlist in the crusading army in the twelfth century. It was seen as a type of 'holy war', rather like the Muslim *jihad*. Contemporaries also used the term *peregrinatio*,[7] which means 'pilgrimage', a term that originally referred to a spiritual pilgrimage, a common event all over medieval Europe undertaken by pilgrims who travelled, usually on foot, to any one of a number of shrines. Crusaders seem to have used the term to emphasize the spiritual nature of their otherwise military undertaking.

Muslims knew the crusading armies collectively as Franks,[8] meaning northern Europeans, after the Frankish soldiers who resisted Muslim incursion into Europe in the eighth century.

The crusades were international affairs, involving most of the countries of Christian Europe, and it could be suggested that the crusades mark a defining moment in the development a collective European identity. The crusades also represent a crucial point in the relationship between Christianity and Islam, creating a rift that may never be closed. For the Christian, joining a crusade was for the glory of God and the good of the individual's soul, and those enlisting were promised spiritual rewards for serving with the Christian army, and the status of Martyr if they died whilst on campaign. Papal letters sent out to archbishops asking them to organize recruitment for a holy war spelt out these privileges in detail. Death on the crusade was deemed to be the equivalent of martyrdom: the soldier would go straight to heaven, and his soul would be spared Purgatory, because this was a war sanctioned by God. In order to get over the normal Christian prohibition against spilling blood, soldiers were reassured that, as St Bernard pointed out in *The New Knighthood*, it was not a sin to spill non-Christian blood.

If this was a war sanctioned by God, contemporaries asked, why did the crusades so often fail, and the Christian army lose battles? Western theologians had to explain away massive Christian defeats such as the Battle of the Horns of Hattin, when people asked the question: where was God when his soldiers were slain? Failure, the theologians suggested, was the result of moral backsliding and sin on the part of the Christian army. This tied in with attitudes in the East towards the Knights Templar whose moral failings were blamed for many of the crusading failures. This contributed to their unpopularity once they had left the Holy Land, and to their eventual downfall.

The type of man the Church hoped would take the cross was strong, trained to arms, and preferably from the knightly class, so able to pay for his own horse, armour, and travel. It was even better if he could bring armed tenantry with him to swell the army. Those who took the cross were whipped up by enthusiastic orators who appealed to their piety, stressing the spiritual rewards they would get such as absolution from their sins, and the parlous state of their brother Christians in Palestine. But there were those who were genuinely motivated by personal piety; many of these joined the military religious orders such as the Knights Templar so that they could demonstrate their devotion to God through poverty, chastity and obedience.

The Crusaders and Islam

The crusaders knew what they were fighting for and why, but what did they know about Islam? Their idea of the Muslims, their religion and civilization was coloured by the propaganda of the pope and his preachers who wanted to spur them on to take the cross and fight in the Holy Land, and by Christian chroniclers who portrayed the Muslims in the worst possible light.

Pope Urban, who sent the first crusade to re-capture Jerusalem, played on the imagination of those who heard or read his sermons by describing the Muslims as barbarians who raped Christian women, murdered Christian children and desecrated Christian churches. Bishop Altmann of Passau described how 'pagans' captured an abbess whilst she was on pilgrimage and in the sight of her fellow pilgrims raped her until she died.[9] Much of the language used about the Muslims in the chronicles is the same as that used about Viking invaders in earlier centuries. Both were unknown heathen enemies threatening Christendom, dragons come to destroy the world.

The rank-and-file crusader knew nothing about Islamic civilization, its religion and holy books, and it was not until the twelfth century that Western scholars had access to a Latin translation of the Koran. Mohammad was described in chronicles and theological works as a false god, while the importance of Jerusalem to Islam was of no concern to the crusaders.

However, Islam also had stereotypes of the crusaders. They were seen as violent and bloodthirsty, killing without mercy, and the West was perceived as a dangerous place where a god-fearing Muslim should fear to go. But animosity towards the West and its crusaders was not on the same level of virulence as that of the Christian chroniclers, although both Muslim and Christians recorded the atrocities of war by the opposing side: they told of prisoners given safe conducts and then slaughtered, of women and children butchered or sold into slavery, promises broken and treaties ignored. The crusade was a holy war for both East and West, and both sides felt that God was on their side. Neither the Christian crusader nor the Muslim knew much about their enemy as an individual person. Not only was there an almost insurmountable language barrier, but propaganda machines of both sides created an atmosphere of fear and hate which prevented barriers between Muslim and Christian being crossed, or either side gaining an understanding of the other.

The Crusader States or 'Outremer'[10]

The Christian crusaders were not entirely unsuccessful, and when they conquered an area they took it into their own hands and set up a Western

---

Box 2.1 The Crusader States

Name	Date of foundation
County of Edessa	1098
Principality of Antioch	1098
Kingdom of Jerusalem	1099
County of Tripoli	1109
Kingdom of Acre	1187
Kingdom of Cyprus	1191

---

state (see Box 2.1), dividing the spoils between the commanders. These states remained separate, thus creating a situation that would lead to conflict between the crusader states as well as between Christian and Muslim within the population. The rulers of these states, were, like the original Knights Templar, of French or Norman origin.[11] The kings of Jerusalem were descendants of the counts of Boulogne, and the prince of Antioch came from Norman Sicily, the counts of Tripoli was descended from the counts of Toulouse and the counts of Edessa from the counts of Corbeil. The crusader states were autonomous and each had its own local customs, but there was an essential similarity, and government for all crusader states was founded on the same feudal law as existed in France and Normandy at the time of the First Crusade. Feudal obligations bound all the tenants of the states; for lords this meant military service for the state's ruler, but whereas the peasants in western Europe were required to do labour service on their lord's land, in the crusader states a system of share-cropping was used whereby a percentage of each year's produce was paid to the lord. In both West and East estates or *fiefs* had to be big enough to supply the ruler with an efficient standing army, so that for those who were granted fiefs there was a material as well as a spiritual reward for crusading.

The new barons of fiefs took over mixed populations of Greek Orthodox Christians, Armenians and Roman Catholics as well as the Muslim native population. The latter outnumbered the other groups. This predominance of the Muslims in the crusader states led the lords to build large castles to protect their interests, and to confine the friendly non-military population to walled towns. They needed settlers from the West to colonize the land and farm it. Some pilgrims and crusaders took up offers of land, but the crusader states were hostile and dangerous environments for Europeans, and luring Western farmers and peasants to cultivate the land proved to be impossible.

The rulers of the crusader states were Roman Catholics, who needed to attract churchmen to serve their spiritual needs. French or Norman priests were the obvious choice, and new bishoprics had to be established to attract high calibre men. Appointments to the new bishoprics were made by the heads of state rather than by the pope, which created a precedent. Churchmen in the crusader states had to deal with countless pilgrims, who wanted to see the sites where Christ had lived and died, and wanted shrines where they could worship and touch relics of Christ's life. A massive church-building programme was undertaken. The Church of the Holy Sepulchre, completed in 1149, was the most holy site.

Pilgrims helped to boost the economy of the crusader states, with their need for food, drink, overnight lodging and guides and they were also inveterate souvenir-hunters. so it was important to keep them safe. This meant that the Knights Templars' role in protecting pilgrims was doubly important. Some hospitality was offered by the monastic foundations, which tended to be situated in towns, it being too dangerous to build them in the countryside. A few contemplative orders took root in the crusader states after the First Crusade, but these disappeared after Saladin's conquest in the late twelfth century.

The crusaders were a colonizing force and their architecture as seen in castles was alien to the area. It was constructed of stone rather than the mud brick of the native houses, and it was based on designs brought from the crusaders' Europe homelands. Many settlements had been destroyed in the prolonged fighting, and the land reverted to desert. The Templars were given permission to build and settle these desolate places, and they carried this settlement pattern through to Europe, for example creating Temple Bruer in Lincolnshire out of desolate heath.

The conquerors and the conquered remained separated by language, and that included the native Christians as well as the Muslims. They were also separated by ideals and expectations, by lifestyle, dress and architecture. The crusader rulers imposed their own laws on the new states. Their marriages were made with other crusader families, and there was little contact with their subjects.

The crusader states were an artificial construct on a shaky foundation, and one by one they fell. Edessa was lost in 1144, Jerusalem in 1187, Antioch in 1263, Tripoli in 1289 and Acre in 1291. The fall of Acre, the last-remaining state, heralded the fall of the Knights Templar whose fortunes in the East were bound up with the crusader states. They had provided the military backbone for these Christian outposts for nearly two centuries, but by 1291 that was all over.

The Cost of Crusading

The aim of the Templars was to keep a flow of money and resources going to the Holy Land, and we should consider how much it cost to send and equip a knight to fight in the East. In order to go on crusade secular knights often had to sell or mortgage their land and pledge their belongings to fund themselves, bringing considerable hardship to their families.[12] Papal taxes helped to fund the second and third crusades; the 1188 Saladin Tithe extracted one-tenth of everyone's income, except that of the Templars; and in 1199 the clergy had to pay one-fortieth of their income to subsidize crusaders, followed by a further twentieth in 1215.

J.P. Richard suggests that it is 'impossible' to estimate the cost to the individual of taking the cross. The expenses would have included equipment and horses, weapons and food, as well as paying for the passage to Palestine. Richard shows that the transport tariff from Venice to Palestine was: two-and-a-half marks (33s 4d) for a knight; and four-and-a-half marks (53s 4d) for a horse. This would have been the basic fare for an individual knight, but he might well have been taking an esquire, foot soldiers and servants with him. It was not unknown for contingents to hire a whole ship that would cost about 1,500 marks or 1,000 pounds.[13]

Before setting out the crusader had to make sure he had adequate equipment. His armour would have been chain mail with a padded surcoat over the top, and a flat-topped helmet. When it was found that Saracen arrows could pierce chain mail, plate armour was added to vulnerable areas such as the knees and shoulders.

Another expense was the horse and its fodder. Experience in the East showed that the light Arab or Barbary steed fared better than the heavy European war horse. Each horse needed about 24lbs of food each day. Grazing was short in the East, so the fodder, usually oats, had to be purchased and carried in wagons or on pack animals. Water was also a problem. Horses needed to be watered at regular intervals, so any march had to go via water courses, and there was always a danger of ambush whilst watering the animals. Horseshoes had to be purchased in bulk and carried with the army.

Some food for the men was purchased before setting out for the East. Richard I purchased cheese from Essex, 14,000 pigs from Hampshire, Essex and Lincolnshire, and dried peas from Cambridgeshire and Kent.[14] Once in the Holy Land more provisions had to be purchased, and each crusader was expected to carry enough provisions with him for a day or two on campaign. This would included biscuits, flour, wine and pork. Put together with cheese and dried pulses made for though possibly necessary to replace salts fost in perspiration very salty diet, which may have

TABLE 2.1 ◆ *Louis IX's Expenditure for Crusading in the Holy Land in 1252*

	Pounds	Shillings	Pence
Food	31,595	11	10
Clothes	104	12	9
Mantles for knights and clerics	312	10	0
Armour for knights	12,910	8	11
Gifts of robes & silver	771	10	0
Crossbowmen and sergeants	4,494	6	6
115 horses & mules	1,916	18	11
Knights' wages	57,093	17	10
Subsidies for volunteer knights	23,253	18	4
Mounted crossbowmen	22,242	13	6
264 replacement horses	6,789	17	0
Foot crossbowmen	29,575	0	6
Engineers	689	12	5
Labourers, guards and ransoms	66,793	19	6
Shipping	5,725	15	0

Total costs for the crusade £2,657,905 16 s 7 d.[15]

caused problems in the East where the sun was hot and water scarce, and dehydration must have always been a problem. Table 2.1 illustrates the expense and resources needed to keep a crusading army in the field.

Notes

1 Nasir-l'-Khresam, quoted in E. Hallam (ed.), *Chronicles of the Crusades, Eyewitness Accounts of the Wars Between Christianity and Islam*, London: Weidenfield and Nicolson (1989), p. 29.

2 Robert the Monk, *Historia Hiersolymitana* , quoted in Hallam, p. 90.

3 J. Riley-Smith, *What Were the Crusades?* London: Macmillan (1977), pp. 21–3.

4 T. Madden (ed.), *The Crusades*, London: Duncan Bird (2004), p. 37.

5 Madden, p. 45.

6 Gerald of Wales *The Journey Through Wales/The Description of Wales* (ed.. and trans. Lewis Thorpe), Harmondsworth: Penguin Classics (1978), pp. 32–3.

7 P. Lock, *The Routledge Companion to the Crusades*, London: Routledge (2006), 289.

8 Lock, 289

9 Quoted in Hallam, 36

10 The Crusader states were also referred to by Europeans as Outremer or 'states beyond the sea'.

11 The Normans were originally Viking stock, and the Duchy of Normandy was an autonomous state in what is now France at the time of the First Crusade. The dukes of Normandy were also kings of England. There were in addition Norman rulers in Sicily.

12 Paris, M. (1984), *Chronicles*, ed. & trans. R. Vaughan, Gloucester: A. Sutton, 206

13 Richard, J.P. (1999), *The Crusades c 1071-c1291*, Cambridge: CUP, 271–279

14 Richard, p. 227.

15 Extracts from the accounts of Louis IX, king of France, in E. Hallam (1989) *Chronicles of the Crusades*, London: Weidenfeld & Nicolson, 270. Louis's accounts have been converted into pounds, shillings and pence, by Hallam.

CHAPTER 3

• • • • • • • • • • • • • • •

Exploits in the East

Hugh de Payens was back in Jerusalem from the Council or Troyes by 1130. As well as the Knights Templar in Jerusalem there was another band of knights there, based at the Hospital of St John. They had been founded to give hospitality to pilgrims, but by 1139 they too were to have a military role. The Knights Templar and the Knights Hospitaller were both rivals and allies. In battle the Knights Templar traditionally led the vanguard and the Knights Hospitaller provided the rearguard. Between them they could mount 600 knights in the field, as well as the sergeants and turcopoliers.

In 1139 the Hospitallers were given the castle of Bethgibelin near the city of Ascalon. This acquisition marked the beginning of the great chain of Templar and Hospitaller castles guarding the pilgrim routes and the approaches to Jerusalem (Map 3.1).

Templar Castles in the East

Templar castles were magnificent constructions, placed strategically on the highest point of the landscape and built of the best quality stonework. These edifices had to serve a dual purpose. They were military garrisons, but also religious houses where the Templars could pursue their life of holy devotion when not on campaign. Inside the castles the forbidding tower-keeps with their arrow-slit windows gave way to the delicate ribbed vaulting of the chapels.

Castles had two practical military functions. One was defensive: to protect the inhabitants during an enemy attack and siege. The other was

MAP 3.1 ◆ *Templar and battle sites in the Kingdom of Jerusalem*

offensive, providing a base from which an aggressive force could issue to attack the enemy. Castles also had a symbolic significance. They reminded those who saw them of that power and domination over the landscape and the people in it. Examples of this are the massive blank walls of the Templar castle Chastel Blanc in Modern-day Syria, which still glowers over the village of Safita below, or Chastel Pelerin (Castle Pilgrim) which could accommodate 4,000 men and had corridors down which an armed knight could ride. This castle stood on a rocky outcrop protecting the coast between Caesarea and Acre.

Templar castles were a sign of the colonization of the Holy Land by a foreign power and culture, and represented the oppression of the non-Christian majority population by a ruling minority. Their construction – the carefully cut stone blocks and the architectural design mirroring that of the Templars' homelands had no echoes in the small settlements around them. The castles were built to impress. A great deal of money and labour, most of it slave labour, went into their building, and the castles came to be seen as symbols of the Knights Templars' pride.

To the south-east of Jerusalem, Le Toron des Chevaliers (The Knights Tower) guarded the city's southern approaches. Further north was the castle of La Fève described by the Saracens, when they took it in 1187, as the best in area. Inland castles included Beaufort and Saphet. The Knights Templar also had fortified towers guarding river crossings and mountain passes. They guarded the town of Gaza and had a fortified citadel at Acre.

These castles, solidly built and strategically placed should have been impregnable, but they fell to the enemy with monotonous regularity. Chronicles claim that when La Fève was taken the Knights Templar in it were killed, whilst the rest of the garrison bribed their way to safety using the Templars' treasures. Saphet was noted for its size, but like other castles it too fell to invaders; taken by the Egyptian slave-turned-general Baybars in 1266. He promised the Templars safe conduct if they surrendered. But as they left the castle they were taken prisoner and executed; 150 knights died and about 700 others were taken prisoner.

This treachery highlights one of the problems faced by the Templars when garrisoning their castles – manpower. The greater part of the garrison was likely to be mercenaries whose loyalty was mainly to their own skins. The castles alone could not win back lost territory for the Christians or keep the enemy at bay. What was needed was a concentrated effort by the combined forces of the military orders, the armies of the crusader states, and reinforcement from the West. It was time for a crusade bringing in Christian knights from across Christendom.

The Second Crusade 1145–9

The Second Crusade was necessary because the leaders of Islam had united under Nur ad-Din with the aim of ridding Palestine of a common enemy, the Christians. The Christians were disunited and riven by discord and rivalry and in 1144 Nur ad-Din conquered the County of Edessa. The military orders sent anguished letters to Pope Eugenius III about their plight, and he sent out a call for a crusade to Louis VII of France. Louis enlisted the help of St Bernard of Clairvaux who on 31 March 1146 at Vezelay in France preached a sermon exhorting men to take up the cross and save both Christendom and their own souls. Thousands were inspired by his oratory and took the cross. Louis and his queen Eleanor of Aquitaine left for the East in May 1147 followed by a fleet bearing the English contingent.

The second crusade moved the Knights Templar into an important and powerful position in the East, as advisers on strategy. When on the march in the East the Templars took the lead, and provided mounted scouts protecting the side of the column. Everard des Barres, the Grand Master during the Second Crusade, divided the column into corps of 50, who could turn outwards and repel attacks, whilst their colleagues rallied to them. Des Barres became King Louis' most trusted adviser, and it was Des Barres who lent Louis money to enable him to carry on with the crusade.[1]

Unfortunately it was also the Knights Templar who were blamed for the failure of the Second Crusade because of the part they allegedly played in the attack on Damascus in July 1149. There is no evidence that they were in fact to blame, but a scapegoat was needed to explain the Damascus disaster, and the Templars were already exciting jealousy amongst their allies.

The attack on Damascus had begun well. The crusaders were encamped to the west of the city in an orchard where there was shade and water, but on 27 July 1149 they moved to the east of the city where there was neither shade nor water, and they were forced to withdraw the next day. The logic behind the move is not recorded, but the Templars quickly got the blame for giving bad advice. William of Tyre, Wibald Abbot of Corvey, John of Wurzberg and John of Salisbury all accused the Templars of treachery at Damascus in 1148. The Wurzburg Chronicler went so far as to accuse the Templars of taking a bribe from the citizens of Damascus to move the crusaders into an untenable position. William of Tyre put it down to the Templars' pride, lack of humility and disobedience.[2] Some of these authors had hidden agendas in blaming the Templars. William of Tyre hated the Order and saw it as a rival to his power. The Abbot of Corvey and John of Wurzberg wanted to show their support for King Conrad of Germany, and to exonerate Louis of France from blame. John of Salisbury repeated gossip he had heard from other sources.

The Templars were to be accused of greed and deceit a few years later at the siege of Ascalon in 1153.[3] A freak accident occurred when the Muslim defenders set light to a siege tower placed against the city walls in the Templars' section, and the heat breached their own walls. The Knights Templar took advantage of this to enter the city, while (allegedly) the rest kept the remainder of the Christian army at bay. According to William of Tyre this was so that the Templars could grab the best of the booty. In the event 40 knights were trapped and killed in the city, and their bodies hung over the walls. Tyre's accusations are not reinforced by other writers, and the city eventually fell to the Christians.

Although Ascalon was taken, Islamic unity and strength was growing under the charismatic leader Saladin, who had taken over when Nur ad-Din died in 1174. Saladin, a Kurd born in about 1137, was an astute politician and strategist. He entered the state service of Egypt and in 1169 became commander of the Egyptian army and vizier of Egypt. Under his command Syria and Palestine were taken into Egyptian control. He died in 1193 and was buried in Damascus. The verdict of his Islamic contemporaries was that he was a failure because he had not been able to take Tyre and had lost ground to the crusaders in the Third Crusade, but he was esteemed by his Christian enemies in the West, and seen as a charismatic leader.[4]

The Affair of the Assassins' Envoy

Saladin made alliances in Palestine and Byzantium that isolated the Crusader states, and led to some strange negotiations for allies. In 1173 talks started between Amalric, king of Jerusalem and the Assassins. The Assassins were an extremist Islamic sect who believed that if they obeyed their leader, known to the West as the Old Man of the Mountains, they would be rewarded in Paradise. They would murder to order, or commit suicide on the instant if he commanded it. They were a fanatical and dangerous sect which survived in Iran and Syria until destroyed by the Mongols in 1256, and in Egypt until 1272.

Fact and fiction mingle about the fate of the Assassin envoy to Jerusalem. William of Tyre claimed that travelling back to the Assassin headquarters the envoy was ambushed by the Knights Templar near Tripoli and killed. Tyre saw this as an act of treason against the king of Jerusalem. Amalric tried to arrest Walter de Mesnil, the Templar respons-ible, but was prevented by the Grand Master. Strife between the king of Jerusalem and the Knights Templar followed. Tyre believed that this brought the Kingdom of Jerusalem to the brink of disaster.[5] However, we must remember Tyre's dislike of the Order, and that he was acting as Amalric's mouthpiece, trying to convince the rest of Christendom that an alliance with a sect so distasteful as the Assassins was for the good of Jeru-salem. Another version of the story, even more damning to the Templars, comes from Walter Map. He suggested that the Old Man of the Mountains wanted to convert to Christianity and that was why the envoy went to Jerusalem, in order to find priests and holy scriptures. Map claims that the Templars killed the envoy because conversion would remove the reason for the war with Islam, and also removed the Templars' source of wealth, plunder taken in battle.[6] There is however no evidence that this suggestion bore any relation to the truth. Other possible explanations might include religious scruples on the part of the Templars about an alliance with the Assassins, or a case of mistaken identity. Indeed, the Templars may not have been responsible for the murder at all, but merely a convenient scapegoat.

The Springs of Cresson and the Horns of Hattin

The clash between Amalric and Odo de St Armand, the Grand Master at that time, illustrates the power and influence of the Grand Master as a figurehead, and how much of the Templars' policy and actions depended on his personality; a fact that was to become even more obvious in the last days of the Templars. It also illustrates how dangerous it was for the Christians to be divided amongst themselves, especially when the combined Islamic army under Saladin was on the march; Acre, Ascalon, Beirut, Gaza and Sidon fell to Saladin, and Jerusalem would be next unless he could be stopped.

Amalric died in 1177 and the succession to the Kingdom of Jerusalem was disputed. So there was no unity amongst the Christian forces when Saladin invaded the kingdom. A truce was declared but this was broken in 1182, and Saladin, now master of Egypt, came back in 1183. Another truce was made between him and the Christians, which lasted until 1187 when a caravan of traders on the road from Cairo to Damascus was attacked by Christians. War followed, and with it a period of disaster and death for the Knights Templar.

The opening act of this dark era took place in front of the Templar castle of La Fève, which the Grand Master Gerard de Ridefort had garrisoned with Templars and Hospitallers from across the region. La Fève was in an excellent strategic position. It lay on a rise commanding the roads to Tiberias, Acre and Jerusalem. It had a good water supply, and at this time enough supplies to withstand a lengthy siege.

On 1 May 1187 de Ridefort and his force rode out to attack Saladin's army at the Springs of Cresson to the north-east of Nazareth. But de Ridefort had underestimated Saladin's strength. He should have stayed behind his castle walls. The Christian army was defeated.

Elsewhere Guy, king of Jerusalem was mustering an army to relieve Tiberias which Saladin had under siege. Saladin's army numbered about 30,000, while Guy could only muster half of that number. But he set out with Templars in their traditional position in the vanguard. The army assembled at Acre on 1 July 1187, and on 2 July Guy's army was encamped at Seppharis on a shady and well-watered site. The king had the option of staying there and waiting for Saladin to attack. But Gerard de Ridefort gave other advice. He said that the Christians and especially the Templars would be dishonoured if they did not move forward and attack. On 3 July Guy led the army away from the shade and water of Seppharis into the arid desert, where they were encircled by Saladin's army. After a night of extreme thirst for men and horses, the crusader army fled for refuge to the twin hills known as the Horns of Hattin. Here Saladin's mounted archers took a dreadful toll on the Christian knights and their horses, before the Muslin cavalry and their scimitars moved in. The Christian army was annihilated. Guy surrendered; Gerard de Ridefort was taken prisoner; and 300 Templar knights were killed in the battle or taken prisoner and executed.

The seeds of the long-term fate of the Knights Templar were sown that hot day on the Horns of Hattin, and the Kingdom of Jerusalem was doomed. Acre fell to Saladin on 10 July and Jerusalem was lost in October 1187. The Templars' original home in the Temple was now in other hands, and those of the Christian population of the city who were too poor to pay for a safe-conduct were sold into slavery.

News of the disaster at the Horns of Hattin quickly spread to Europe. It was dispersed throughout Christendom by papal letters to archbishops and reports sent back to European princes by their subjects who had been in the East at the time. A new crusade to win back Jerusalem was desperately needed.

The Third Crusade

The Third Crusade was led by Richard I of England and Philip II of France. They had an uneasy relationship as France and England had been at war shortly before the Third Crusade was preached. On his way east Richard conquered Cyprus. He sold the island to the Templars for 25,000 marks. They re-sold it a year after to Guy of Lusignan. It was claimed that during the Templars' ownership they levied extortionate taxes and oppressed the population. This was the start of their troubled relationship with the island. A third Western leader arrived in the East at this time, Frederick Barbarossa of the Holy Roman Empire, who was accompanied by the Teutonic knights. He was drowned on 10 June 1190.

The Third Crusade took back Acre for the Christians, and Richard desperately wanted to push on to Jerusalem. Harried by the Saracens, short of food and water and realising that even if he took Jerusalem he would not be able to keep it, Richard withdrew to Jaffa. The momentum went out of the crusade. Richard fell ill and when he recovered he agreed to a truce with Saladin, and started home. The Third Crusade was seriously impaired by the rivalry and lack of communication between the leaders, and little was achieved. Saladin died in 1193, Richard in 1199.

The Fourth Crusade

In 1200 Pope Innocent III produced propaganda for a new crusade that would outstrip all previous efforts, win back Jerusalem and put the crusader states on a firm footing. His plan was to sail directly to Egypt and secure what was seen as the main Islamic power base there. The Republic of Venice would supply transport.

Innocent III tried to make it clear that this time there would be no rivalry between the leaders or turning the Knights Templar into scapegoats. He pointed out that the Templars were under his protection, but also that any abuses by the Templars must cease. The Fourth Crusade was diverted from its purpose to Constantinople, whilst the Templars and the other military orders tried to keep some control of territory in the Holy Land.

The Fifth Crusade

In 1216 a new pope Honorius III promoted a new crusade. The Fifth Crusade drew contingents from England, France, Austria and the Low countries. The crusade focused its efforts on Egypt as a starting-point for the recapture of the Holy Land. Its first objective was to take Damietta on the Nile delta, which was on the direct route to Cairo. The crusaders attacked by sea, but could not take the city, and a siege followed. The city fell to the Christian army in November 1219 and was sacked by the crusaders.

Taking the city was one thing, holding it was another. The Templars who helped to garrison the city began to express doubts about the whole campaign and the wisdom of pressing on into Egypt. Cardinal Pelagius, the crusade's nominal leader, argued for an advance. The military orders and the lay commanders opposed this, suggesting that it would be prudent to wait until the arrival of the Emperor Frederick II and his force. Despite this the order to advance was given. Perhaps the cardinal acted because of murmurings in the West that the crusade had reached a stalemate. The Egyptians, seeing the crusaders preparing to advance, opened sluice gates and blockaded river access to the town. Short of food and cut off from supplies the crusaders were forced to accept a truce. Damietta was lost. Had the Emperor Frederick II arrived with his promised force it might have been held, but Frederick did not reach the East until 1228.

It was during Frederick's sojourn that Western politics impinged on the East, and threatened what little stability the Christians had in the area. Frederick had been preceded by papal letters telling the Christians to have nothing to do with him, as he had been excommunicated over a long-running dispute in Sicily. The Templars, who owed allegiance to the pope, obeyed. Frederick, used to power politics in the West and absorbing all important sites into his own hands, promptly asked them to surrender the castle at Atlit to him. They refused. He then laid siege to their commandery at Acre, and started a propaganda war against them. He spread it about that the pope, the Knights Templar and the sultan of Egypt were plotting to murder him. Counter-propaganda against Frederick reached England and was recorded by Matthew Paris:

> In these days the face of Frederick began to be much despised throughout the different regions of the world, he was now reckoned to be worse than Herod, Judas or Nero for the deadly stench given out by his deeds.

He quotes in full the text of a letter from Cardinal Reiner of Viterbo to the pope detailing Frederick's iniquities.[7]

Frederick retook Jerusalem, staying in the city for two days before negotiating a truce and agreeing that it should remain unfortified. He then returned to Sicily, confiscated all the property belonging to the Templars and Hospitallers and threw the occupants into gaol.

Internal strife kept the Knights Templar busy until 1240. The Hospitallers, who had originally supported the Templars against Frederick, moved to the Imperialist side, and in October 1241 the Templars besieged the Hospitallers' house in Acre. These squabbles between the military orders, and the imperialist ambitions of Frederick and his rivals, helped to destroy the Christian kingdoms in the Holy Land. Outrage about the situation came west with the crusaders returning from Richard of Cornwall's crusade of 1241. Further discredit fell on the Templars in 1244 when a conflict between Salih Aiyub and Ismail of Damascus broke out. The Templars advised supporting the latter with the result that Aiyub made an alliance with the Turks and attacked Damascus. This was followed by an attack on Jerusalem, and on 11 July 1244 Jerusalem was taken by the Turks and sacked. Christian rule would not return to the Holy City.

The Christian army decided to meet a combined force of Turks and Egyptians in open battle at La Forbie near Gaza on 17 October 1244. The Christian army was defeated. The Templar Grand Master was either captured or killed and only 33 out of 300 Templar knights survived. Frederick II gleefully blamed the disaster on the Templars, suggesting that their aggression towards Egypt had propelled Egypt into the Turks' arms.

Louis IX's First Crusade

Response from the West to the fall of Jerusalem was slow in coming, indicating a decline in interest in the East and a preoccupation with events at home. Nevertheless, King Louis IX of France took the cross in 1244, although he did not actually set out on his crusade until August 1248. When he reached Cyprus he stayed there until May 1249, eventually landing in Egypt on 5 June 1249. Whilst Louis was on Cyprus, Matthew Paris suggests that 'the king of France, following sane and saintly advice, fully pacified many nobles in dispute, including the Templars and the Hospitallers, both in Cyprus and other parts of the Christendom . . .'[8]

By September 1249 Paris reported that the crusaders had taken Damietta.[9] The crusaders left Damietta in January 1250 and advanced towards Cairo. On 7 February 1250 the crusaders crossed the Mansurah canal and led by Louis's brother Robert of Artois advanced on the town of Mansurah; and on the 8th they crossed the Bedouin ford. Jean de Joinville takes up the story:

> Orders were given that the Templars should have the vanguard and that
> the Count of Artois should lead the second squadron after the Templars.
> When Artois crossed the ford he came upon about 300 Turkish horsemen
> that he routed. The Templars sent word that he had treated them very
> scurvily when he was to have gone after them and not before; and they
> begged him to let them go first, as had been agreed by the king. Now it so
> befell that Artois did not answer them, because my lord Foucauld de
> Merle, that held his horse, and this Foucauld, who was a very good old
> knight heard nothing that the Templars said to the County [Count], for
> he was deaf, and cried 'At them! Now at them!'

*When the Templars saw this, they thought themselves that they
would be dishonoured if they let the Count of Artois go before them; so
they set spur to their horses, every man with all his might, and gave
chase to the Turks who fled before them into the fields beyond Mansurah
and towards Cairo. When they thought to turn back the Turks cast beams
and boards into the streets upon them . . . The Count of Artois met his
death . . . The Templars as the Master has told me since lost fourteen
score armed men and horses and all mounted.*[10]

Three hundred secular knights were lost and 280 Templars and their
horses. The loss of manpower was tragic and the loss of 600 horses
disabled the crusader army. Were the Templars to blame as Joinville
suggested? Matthew Paris had a different version, although we must
remember that Joinville was present, while Paris was not. Paris suggests
that Artois was proud and arrogant and wished to carry off the honour for
himself; that he routed the Turkish horsemen and said to the Master of
the Temple that they should follow up the enemy and crush them.

*To this the master of the knights of the Temple, a discreet and wary
man skilled in military affairs replied, 'My lord and noble count, we
can commend well enough your efforts, your innate generosity and
your bravery freely devoted to the honour of the Lord and his universal
Church, which we know about and have often experienced. However, we
would like and we advise and entreat you advantageously to restrain this
fervour with the bridle of modesty and honour that the Lord has given us.
For after the heat of battle we are tired, wounded, hungry and thirsty: . . .'*

He suggested waiting until there was further council with king Louis.

*When the Count of Artois heard this he was highly indignant and,
excited and flushed with anger and pride replied, 'See the time-honoured
treachery of the Temple . . . What deceit hidden for a long time, now
appears openly in our midst . . ., [Hearing this the] irate master of the
Temple said angrily to his standard-bearer in a loud voice: 'Unfurl and
raise our banner and we shall advance to battle to experience together
today the uncertain fortunes of war and the chance of death . . .'*[11]

Louis called a council on 9 February, and then set off on the road to
Mansurah. As the Christians advanced they came upon the mutilated

bodies of Artois's force and the Templars. The battle recommenced until sunset, when the king received news of Artois' death. When they came to their camp they found the Saracens there before them, and put them to flight, but as they lay in their tents sleeping the Saracens attacked them in their turn and were beaten off again. The Saracens and Turks came at sunrise on 11 February and charged. In the king's squadron was William of Sonnac, Grand Master of the Temple,

> with such few of his brethren as remained to him after Tuesday's battle. He had caused a fence to be reared in front of the Saracens' engines that we had taken. When the Saracens attacked, they cast Greek fire against the hoarding they had set up; and the fire quickly took . . . And ye know that the Turks did not wait for the fire to be burnt out but charged the Templars through the burning flame. And in this battle Brother William, the Master of the Temple lost an eye; and the other he had lost on Shrove Tuesday.[12]

After the battles 'great ills came to the host; for at the end of none days, the bodies of our men whom they had killed came to the surface of the water . . . they came floating as far as the bridge between the two camps and the stream was full of dead men.' Thirst and famine followed and on 5 April 1250 Louis withdrew towards Damietta. During the withdrawal the king and Joinville were captured and held to ransom. However, the amount was 15,000 crowns short of the full amount demanded. Joinville suggested that they should apply to the Templars for the missing amount. But the Grand Master, blinded at Mansurah, was now dead, and the commander Brother Stephen of Otricourt had no authority to hand over the money. Hard words followed until Brother Reginald de Vichiers came up with the solution that if the French took the money by force the Templars would not be breaking any oaths.[13]

The money was in chests abroad one of the Templars' galleys. Joinville and others 'invaded' the galley and asked for the keys to the chests. When these were refused they picked up a hatchet lying near by and broke open the chests.[14]

Louis left for Cyprus in April 1254. His departure meant that the great age of crusades was over. From this point onwards the Templars and other Latin lords were left hanging on to territory in the Holy Land by their finger tips.

Notes

1 Odo De Deuil, *De perfectione Ludovic VII in Orientem*, New York: Records of Civilization, Sources and Studies (1948), vii, pp. 132–5.

2 John of Wurzburg, *Descriptiones Terrae Sanctae ex saec*, ed. T. Tobles, Leipzig (1874); John of Salisbury, *Historia pontificalis*, ed. & trans. M. Chibnall (1956), p. 57; William of Tyre, *A History of Deeds Done Beyond the Sea*, trans, E.A. Babcock and A.C. Krey, New York: Columbia University Press (1943), 1, for example p. 526.

3 Note that both this and the preceding incident took place in July with heat and dust at their highest. Surely not a good season for campaigning and perhaps evidence of more bad advice. Some secondary sources put the siege in August, for example M. Barber, *The New Knighthood*, Cambridge: CUP (1994), pp. 74–5; John France dates it to July: J. France, 'Impelled by the Love of God', in T. Madden (ed.), *The Crusades*, London: Duncan Baird (2004), p. 52. Similarly Barber dates the fall of Ascalon to 22 August, France to 19 August.

4 P. Lock, *The Routledge Companion to the Crusades*, London: Routledge (2006), p. 250.

5 Tyre, pp. 953–5.

6 Walter Map, *De nugis curialium*, ed. F.S. Hartland and M.R. James, Cymmrodian Record Series (1923), ix, pp. 66–7.

7 Matthew Paris, *Chronicles of Matthew Paris*, ed. and trans. R. Vaughan, Gloucester: Alan Sutton (1984), pp. 172–3.

8 Paris, p. 181.

9 Paris, p. 188.

10 Joinville, Jean de, *The History of St Louis*, trans N. de Wailly and J. Evans, Oxford: OUP (1938), pp. 64–5.

11 Paris, pp. 239–47.

12 Joinville, pp. 76–81.

13 Reginald (or Reynald) de Vichiers, who helped the king pay his ransom, became the next Grand Master and was at Louis' side during lengthy negotiations with the Saracens.

14 Joinville, pp. 110–14.

CHAPTER 4

Medieval Europe at the time of the Knights Templar

Feudal Europe

The quality of life in medieval Europe at the time of the Knights Templar depended on social status, and where in the social hierarchy a person had been born. Although there were variations, most of twelfth-century Europe was a feudal society in which social relationships were based on property, service and obligation. This was the model of society that the crusaders took east, and the organization of the Knights Templar itself was based on feudalism.

Feudalism tied society together by a series of obligations, interdependence and servitude. It produced a pyramid-shaped society with the monarch or overlord at the apex, and the nobility and knightly class forming the next level. The early Knights Templar came from this class. They were tied to their overlord by providing military service as required, in return for estates known as fiefs. The fief was divided into manors, and these could be sub-let (sub-infeudated) to sub-tenants who owed service to the head of the fief in the same way as he owed service to his overlord.

The manors provided income for the lord of the manor, and also manpower in the form of serfs (unfree peasants) tied to the manor by labour obligations, which usually involved working on the lord's land for a given number of days a week or year, plus 'rent' in kind. In return serfs were allocated strips in the manor's fields to cultivate, and given the nominal protection of their lord. Although the knights of the Templar

Order came from the landowning section of society, the sergeants and lay servants would have come from the class that lay between the lords of the manor and the serfs – freemen, who were members of the lesser landowning class of sub-tenants.

This system can also be seen in the 1185 Inquest of the Templar lands in England. The inquest shows who gave the Templars the land in the first place. This could be the king, for example King Stephen gave the Templars Witham and Cressing Temple in Essex, or a great baron, such as Count Gilbert who gave the Templars Baldock in Hertfordshire.[1] Bernard Balliol also granted the order land in Hertfordshire which was to become Temple Dinsley, the most important commandery in England outside of London.[2] The inquest then lists the who went with the land like movable goods, giving their service requirements and the rent they had to pay (see Box 4.1). Although no similar inquest exists for France the charters granting the Templar's property there included the serfs on the manors.

The serf was tied to the manor and could not leave it without permission, and when the head of the household died the family's best beast had to be given to the lord. This 'entry fine' was known as the heriot. Transactions involving land passing from tenant to tenant took place in the manorial court, and the manorial court oversaw the day-to-day running of the manor, settled disputes amongst tenants, and adjudicated on

---

Box 4.1 Example of Templar tenants at Temple Bruer in Lincolnshire

Hugh Bell for 6 acres and 1 toft 18d, 4 hens and 4 days' labour service

William de Riskintune for 2 bovates and 6 acres with 2 tofts, 7s 6d, 8 hens and 8 days' labour service

William de Schinerde for half a bovate and 1 toft, 2s, 4 hens and 4 days' labour service

Ralph son of Torstan for 6 acres and 1 toft 18d and 4 hens and 4 days' labour service

Roger de Blankenne for 18 acres and 1 toft, 2s 6d, 4 hens and 4 days' labour service

Ailif, widow, for 3 and a half acres 14d and 4 hens and 4 days' labour service[3]

petty crimes such as theft or trespass. Outside the manor the serf could only be represented at a court of law by the lord of the manor. The manorial system extended into the towns, but in the towns there was a larger section of freemen and an embryonic 'Middle class', including merchants, craftsmen and traders.

The feudal system helped to define the structure of society and relationships within it. It defined how the legal system operated, and the responsibilities of each section of society to the other. One of these responsibilities, as we have seen, was to provide military service for the overlord, and feudal society was a society based on arms, so that the Knights Templar as military monks were not out of place.

By the time of the Templars' arrests feudal society was changing. More land was being let for rent alone, and the lord's land was being worked by hired hands. More armies were being raised by 'indentures' and payment rather than by feudal obligation.

The Church

In parallel with secular society was the Church, which in medieval Europe played an important part in the everyday life of lord and peasant alike. Church provinces, sees and religious orders archbishops, bishops, monks and nuns, and at a local level the parish priest ministered to the spiritual needs of his community. In return for this the parishioners were expected to pay one tenth, that is the *tithe*, of their produce or wages. The Templars were exempt from this, which helped to make them unpopular. There is no evidence that the Knights Templar participated in the public activity of the secular Church or in local feasts. But they would have observed them as required, and there is evidence that they sponsored their own fairs, for example at Rothley in Leicestershire, and the 1185 Inquest shows that they observed some local customs, for example paying local taxes in Essex on Hoke Day,[4] the Monday after Easter, the customary day for merriment, feasting and paying dues.

The parish priest was a member of the community, often with a stipend that was little more than the peasant's subsistence income, especially if the tithes were paid to an absentee incumbent, and the vicar was a paid employee. On the other end of the scale were the high churchmen, archbishops, bishops, abbots and abbesses who were as wealthy and powerful as the feudal magnates. They served on the king's council, and acted as diplomats, advisers and friends to the monarch. Like the magnates they might fall from favour, and it was during the Templars' time that Thomas à Becket, the archbishop of Canterbury, was murdered at the (possibly unintentional) instigation of Henry II. One of his murderers was sent off to join the Templars as an associate member as part of his penance after absolution.

Absolution from sins could also be gained through pilgrimage. People would save up for years to go on pilgrimage, and for the peasant this represented the only chance for a remission from work and to leave the manor for a holiday. Most could only afford to go on short pilgrimages to shrines in their own country. In England the two most important and popular shrines were the tomb of Thomas à Becket at Canterbury, and the shrine of Our Lady of Walsingham in Norfolk. There were numerous other shrines across the country. Some of these were believed to confer special benefits or to possess special healing powers. On the continent the shrine of St James of Compostella was an important site on the pilgrim route, as was a visit to Rome, but the ultimate goal of the committed pilgrim was Jerusalem.

Pilgrims were an important feature of the medieval economy; not only for the Church, which charged pilgrims a fee to see the relics, but also for the villages and towns which housed the shrines. Pilgrims needed lodgings, food and drink, which boosted the service industry, and pilgrims also wanted souvenirs as evidence that they had completed their pilgrimage – the scallop shell of St James of Compostella is a well-known example of this.

Another important source of income for the Church was the idea of Purgatory. Purgatory was name given to the area where if was believed the soul underwent punishment for its unexpiated sins before entering Heaven. The time spent in Purgatory could be shortened by good works and gifts to the Church or one of its foundations often by the relatives and friends of the departed. This was how the Knights Templar may have obtained much of their property. For example in 1149 Miles, the count of Hereford gave the Knights Templar two hides in Lockeridge, Wiltshire, for the souls of Walter and Berthe his parents, his own soul and the souls of his ancestors and friends.[5]

In their role as a religious order the Templars followed the life of a monk. The religious services would have started at 4 o'clock with the office of Lauds (pure praise). This was followed by Prime or the morning prayers, and Terce at 9 o'clock. Terce was the Roman 'third hour' and celebrated the time that the apostles received the Holy Spirit. Sext was at midday, None at 3 o'clock, Vespers at six and Compline at eight after which monks retired to bed until. Matins which was held at midnight.[6]

No settlement in medieval Europe was far from a religious foundation, be it one of the great Benedictine houses or a small group of Poor Clares. The abbeys and convents provided education for the children of those who could afford it, alms for the poor and medicine for the sick. (The monastic infirmary, however, was for sick monks rather than the community at large, and complaints were made to bishops by monks who had to share their infirmary with outsiders.) One role of the monasteries was to create and copy manuscripts. Although the Knights Templar claimed to be unlettered men, it was the Church and religious foundations that held the gift of reading and writing in their hands, and it is probable that many Templars could read and write. There was at least one Templar poet in England, who lived at Temple Bruer. Another literate Templar was the Templar of Tyre who wrote his own chronicle starting in 1242 and ending in 1309. In this he included a poem which he says he did not write, but which he found after Acre and Syria were lost, and which may have been written by another Templar. The poem, which runs to 54 verses, is a comment on events and a plea that he will be remembered.[7]

European culture at the time of the Templars

The poem included in the *Chronicle of the Templar of Tyre* was in the vernacular (French in this case), and the fourteenth century saw a growth in such vernacular literary works, including those in English by Geoffrey Chaucer, or the anonymous *Sir Gawain and the Green Knight*. The early Templars would have been familiar with troubadours' songs of courtly love, with the *Roman de la Rose*, or the Arthurian epics of Chrétien de Troyes, which extolled the virtues of the perfect knight. Non-fiction works included chronicles, letters and memoirs, description of great events, religious books such as the Bible and the lives of saints, and descriptions of how the liturgy should be conducted. Other manuscripts included music and choir books, 'mirrors' for princes describing how they should behave, and books of hours giving prayers throughout the day. Most of these were in Latin, and all were, of course, handwritten.

Monasteries had teams of scribes copying works, and producing new manuscripts. At a local level there were scribes to write charters transferring land and other legal documents. The parish priest often wrote the last wills and testaments of the wealthier parishioners, whilst the manorial steward or bailiff kept the record of the manorial court and accounts. Beneath the literate culture of the elite was a strong current of oral tradition, story-telling, songs and plays. News about current affairs would have been passed on by word of mouth, as would popular legends and stories.

When the Order of the Knights Templar was founded Western architecture was still characterized by the round Norman or Romanesque arch, with immense round pillars holding up structures such as Durham Cathedral. However, the architecture that the crusaders observed in the East showed that a pointed arch could take strains and stresses as well as or better than the round arch, and looked more elegant. (Some Norman churches collapsed under their own weight as the pillars were faced with worked stone, but filled with rubble.) The style using these pointed arches, known as Early English in England and Gothic on the continent, started to appear in Britain in the late twelfth century.

Some of the Templar churches in Europe had round naves (for example the Temple Church in London) in imitation of the Church of the Holy Sepulchre (though not all round churches are Templar churches), but often these were turned into rectangles in the thirteenth century as fashions and architecture changed. The West Door of the New Temple in London has a Norman/Romanesque round arch, but the round nave has a fusion of Norman and Early English with round-arched windows and stepped buttresses, but a blind arcade of Early English arches. The New Temple was started in 1166 and consecrated in 1185,[8] so these 'Gothic' arches are early examples of the new architectural idiom in England. The choir was not completed until 1240 and is entirely Gothic.

Inside the Templer churches the decoration was often in an Eastern style, carpeted and hung with banners. Decoration included engravings, and at the church of San Bevignate (patron saint of flagellants) in Perugia a series of paintings shows the Templars' exploits in the east. Here we can see them taking ship for the East in a galley flying their black-and-white pennant, and riding into battle. Many of their churches were dedicated to St George, whose knightly exploits had a special resonance for the Order. But most were dedicated to the Virgin Mary, and the cult of the Virgin was extremely strong in the Order, as can be seen from Jacques de Molay's last words when he wished to die looking on her.

One of the most poignant reminders of those who lived at the time of the Templars are the memorials to the dead. These were only for the elite, and could be in stone, brass or wood, and it was possible to bespoke these before death from an order book, so they are not always accurate portraits. There are no Templar memorial effigies, as this would have been against the Order's vow of poverty. The effigies of the knights in the New Temple are associate members, or in the case of Geoffrey de Mandeville, someone who had the Templar mantle thrown over him as he lay dying. De Mandeville had been excommunicated for sacking Ramsey Abbey in Huntingdonshire in 1143. Mortally wounded subsequently at the siege of Burwell Castle in Cambridgeshire, during the civil war between King Stephen and the Empress Hatilda, he asked for the Templar mantle to be thrown over him, so that the Templars could claim him as one of their own. After his death the Templars took him back to the Old Temple in Holborn and hung him, in a lead coffin, from a tree in their orchard. When the New Temple was completed, de Mandeville's excommunication was reversed and he was buried in the nave.[9]

Prior to someone's death the priest would bring the consecrated host to the bedside, hear the last confession and give absolution. A peasant would then have been put in the earth with little ceremony, but the wealthier members of the community would lie in state on a bier surrounded by candles, and were then buried with a requiem mass. If the dead person had given a donation to the church his or her name could be written in an *obit* or bede roll, and prayers would be offered for his or her soul on the anniversary of death. One obit roll for the Templars has survived at Rheims in France. This gives the name of the person to be remembered, lays down when prayers were to be said, and lists what the person gave to the Order. This could be money, land or a gift in kind.

Peasant life at the time of the Knights Templar

Peasants at the time of the Templars were either serfs tied to the manor, or freemen who could buy and sell land, apprentice their sons to a craft, and put their daughters in a nunnery. Even the unfree peasants were divided into 'classes'. Villeins who usually held a viable acreage, the bordars or smallholders who held some land but not always an amount sufficient for their needs, and the cottars who had a cottage and a garden but little else. The cottars sometimes provided labour for the villeins, and the villeins who held land by labour service paid them wages to do this on their behalf.[10] Labour service's could be onerous. They entailed not only working a number of days each week or year on the lord of the manor's land, but also performing other tasks such as taking the manorial produce to market, repairing sheep pens, dipping sheep, or clearing waste land. The amount of labour service required depended on the lord of the manor. In general the Knights Templars' demands were light when compared with other ecclesiastical landlords such as St Albans Abbey.[11]

In addition to regular labour service there was boon work which was required at crisis times in the agricultural year – at haymaking and harvest.

The life of the elite at the time of the Knights Templar

Overall the elite lived in greater comfort than the peasantry.

They drew their income from the land that their serfs worked for them, and did not have to labour for themselves. Instead the men of the family served their overlord by providing men-at-arms and military leadership when necessary, taking on public offices (usually with a handsome stipend), acting as advisers to the monarch and serving in parliament in England and the national assembly in France. They were the monarch's representatives at a local level, dispensing justice and overseeing public works. Their income from land usually amounted to somewhere between £3,000 and £11,000 a year. (This can be compared with the £2 a year the peasant labourer earned.)[12] The elite were also great consumers of goods and chattels, and this helped to fuel the wider economy through their demand for the latest fashions in dress and household goods, and through the large households they supported.

A member of the medieval elite might have multiple residences, including one in the capital city, a strategically placed castle and numerous manor houses. We have seen that the living standard of the elite was vastly different to that of the peasants, but how did the lifestyle of the Knights Templar in Europe compare to this? Were they living in luxury as was suggested at the trial?

Towns at the time of the Knights Templar

The population of medieval Europe at this time was still largely rural, and the economy was based on agriculture. But towns were expanding, and new towns such as the Templar's town of Baldock were being founded. The Order had houses in towns and cities across Europe. This expansion was encouraged by trade, both long-distance and local commercialization, and the gradual emergence of non-agricultural trades.

Medieval towns were usually defended by walls, such as can still be seen at Carcassonne, a prime Templar site in France. Carcassonne consists of two settlements; the old settlement on the hill above the river Aude and the lower town across the river. The lower town was founded in 1240 when the inhabitants of the upper town were expelled by Louis IX and told to build themselves a new settlement. The upper town then became a military citadel.[13]

Urban houses and streets were crowded in behind the town walls, with narrow lanes and alleys, interspersed with public spaces such as the market place. Entry to the town was through guarded gateways that were closed at night. The main streets in some towns were paved or cobbled. Paris streets were paved by 1185, but most towns were unpaved throughout the medieval period. Space was at a premium, so houses were built upwards with projecting upper floors that cut off the light from the street below. A town could be divided into many small parishes each with its own church, as can still be seen in York, for example. Parish life and the Church were as important to the town-dweller as to those in the countryside.

Towns might be governed through a manorial court, or, if the town had a charter, through a mayor and aldermen, or through a religious guild such as the Holy Trinity Guild at Kings Lynn. In large cities such as London each ward had its own local government.

There was a still a strong relationship between the town and the countryside. Most towns had their own fields, commons, woodland and vineyards, and citizens worked to bring in the harvest. Animals roamed the town streets, hay carts blocked the roads, and stables, cowsheds and pig pens were added to houses. These added to the smells and sounds of the town. The medieval town would have smelt of manure and the air and water courses would have been heavily polluted. Sanitation was mostly in the form of cess pits which had to be cleared out or tilled in, although the London Court of Nuisance heard cases where people had erected privies above streams and rivers such as the River Fleet. The Templars were accused of diverting water from the Fleet to their water mill at Baynard's Castle, and impeding access by planting willows along the bank. They added to the pollution with two forges in Fleet Street.[14]

Life in town could be exciting, colourful and violent, but the larger towns could not exist without provisions from the countryside, a demand that was increasing by the time the Templars were suppressed, as the population of towns continued to grow.

Conclusion

Europe at the time of the Templars was a society based on inequality of resources, and the obligation of one sector of society to another. No one section could exist without the other, so that the whole was a web of interconnected relationships. The Knights Templar were part of this system. As feudal lords they had tenants who paid rent and worked on their land, and in return the tenants looked to them for protect. Local court records show that the Knights Templar did indeed try to protect their tenants from incursions by outsiders – sometimes by law and sometimes by force.

Life in town and countryside was regulated by manorial customs and the church. The church marked the time of day, the passing of the seasons, and the three great life-cycle events, birth, marriage and death. Life might be hard, indeed amounting to no more than subsistence for the poor, but it was interspersed with feasts and festivities, and it was not all hard work. Sundays were a day of rest, and saints days and important religious festivals provided holidays.

Written records show us the hardships, famine and disease, murder and violence between neighbours, but what they do not tell us is the joy of young people rising early to gather greenery on May Day, the companionship of the guild feast, or the warmth and sociability of Christmastide. Human emotions cannot be reconstructed from the past, but by piecing together the records and reading contemporary verse and romances, we can imagine what it was like.

Notes

1 The 1185 Inquest is at the National Archives, E 164/16. There is a printed version, but it has not been translated from the Latin in B. Lees, *Records of the Templars in England in the 12th century*, London: British Academy, Records of Economic and Social History of England, IX (1935).

2 On 27 April 1147 wearing the white robes of the Order at least 150 Knights Templar on their way to take part in the Second Crusade gathered in Paris to witness the charter in the presence of the Pope, the King of France, and five archbishops. Lees, pp. 211–16.

3 Lees, pp. 94–5.

4 Lees, p. 9.

5 Lees, p. 207.

6 E. Lord, *The Knights Templar in Britain*, Pearson Education (2004), pp. 270–1.

7 G. Raynaud, *Les Gestes des Chiprois*, Geneva: Jules-Guillaume Ficke (1887), pp. 263–72.

8 E. Lord, pp. 40, 46.

9 E. Lord, p. 32.

10 See F.W. Maitland, *Domesday Book and Beyond*, Cambridge: CUP (1987), pp. 23–6.

11 E. Lord, 'The Knights Templar in Hertfordshire; Landlords and Farmers', *Herts Past and Present* (Autumn 2005).

12 C. Dyer, *Standards of living in the Middle Ages*, Cambridge: CUP (1990), pp. 29, 39, 156–7.

13 A.E.J. Morris, *History of Urban Form before the Industrial Revolution*, Longman (1994, 3rd ed), pp. 122–3.

14 Lord, *Knights Templar in Britain*, pp. 49–51.

CHAPTER 5

. . . .

The Templars in the West

When Hugh de Payens came west he not only sought recognition for his new religious order but he was also in pursuit of resources. He needed revenues to fund the Order's efforts in the East. He needed manpower, arms, horses and supplies. He hoped that Western magnates would take pity on the Order and grant it lands and rents in Europe, the proceeds from which could be sent out East.

In this quest he was helped by the doctrines of the Catholic Church. As we have seen, one of the horrors that the living sought to avoid after death was torment in Purgatory. The length of time spent in Purgatory could be shortened by masses and offices said for the soul, by doing good works, and by the grant of lands and revenues to the Church and its religious foundations. This could be seen as a form of religious blackmail, extorting gifts through the threat of pain to the soul after death; but it was extremely beneficial to an order such as the Knights Templar.

Hugh's appeal offered a chance to redeem time in Purgatory by giving to an organization that the landholder could understand and empathize with. Knights trained in arms were something to which they could relate, and the aim of the Templars in protecting the Holy Land from its enemies was something to which they could subscribe. Furthermore, the vows the Templars took, denying themselves luxury and substituting this for hardship, turned them into surrogate penitents for the rest of the knightly class. Donations of lands, rents, churches, mills and vineyards began to flood in to the Templars from princes and their courts. In addition there were many pious donations, and subsidies given to the Templars by the laity.

The organization of Templar estates in the West

At first the grants of land were random and scattered, but soon the Templars were rationalizing their holdings by a process of purchase and exchange. They consciously acquired land and property along major roads and rivers. In England they had houses along the Thames from Sandford in Oxfordshire to Buckinghamshire, and southwards on to the New Temple and Southwark, Strood and Dartford in Kent. They had houses in major ports such as Dover, Bristol and Shoreham in England, La Rochelle and Marseilles in France, and on the Adriatic. They had houses in Siena and Pisa and a network of commanderies in Tuscany, Apulia and Sicily, the Papal States and Abruzzi. In Iberia they were on the Muslim front line requiring castles and fortified houses. By 1150 in France they had been given estates, churches, fishponds, mills, houses, vineyards, rights to take game, and rents in cash and kind. Membership in the West alone had increased to at least 130 knights. They were scattered across Europe, but with a concentration in the Avignon and Toulouse areas of France.[1] By the thirteenth century their estates had spread into Eastern Europe with property in Poland and Prussia.

As significant landowners the Templars had to organize and manage their scattered but lucrative estates. In order to do this they divided their estates into linguistic provinces, and each province into baileys. Each province had its own master and held provincial chapter meetings. A visitor inspected the Order's houses at regular intervals.

Each province had a central focus, a place such as the London or Paris Temples, as well as commanderies in the countryside of varying importance; for example Temple Dinsley in Hertfordshire which frequently hosted the provincial chapter. Some commanderies were fortified, but usually these were large farmsteads with the addition of a hall, dormitory and chapel. Domestic work in the commanderies and labour on the home farm was done by servants; some of these were members of the Order, others were waged labour, or tenants who held their land by labour service, namely work on the Templars' land. Resident in the larger commanderies were knights and sergeants, and the Templars also had hospitals for elderly brothers such as that at Denny in Cambridgeshire.

The aim of the Templars' estates was to make a profit to send either as cash or produce to the East. As this was the main objective of the Templars' husbandry and management of their estates, it might be expected that they would extract every ounce of sweat from their tenants who held land by labour service, every penny from those paying rent, and strike a hard bargain when marketing their produce. However, there is no evidence that this was the case. The Templars were no harsher landlords than other ecclesiastical or secular landlords, and in fact they were much fairer to their tenants than some.[2]

The great inquest of the Knights Templar holdings in England compiled in 1185 shows that the Templars had revenues that amounted to at least £528 1s 7d a year.[3] The actual amount would have been excess of this figure as it does not take into account rents in kind and labour service provided by the tenants.

There is some evidence that the Templars farmed intensively and made the most of market forces, switching to sheep-rearing when wool commanded a high price or to arable when wheat was in short supply. As relative latecomers to the landed scene both the Templars and the Cistercians were often given land that needed improving or clearing from woodland before it became productive. The Templars undertook programmes of improvement, and gave licences to their tenants to fell trees. At Douzens in France that lay in the disputed land between Toulouse and Barcelona they rationalized their estates into blocks, purchasing and exchanging with neighbouring landowners as necessary. They constructed a number of mills on the river Aude, and leased these out for rent in kind.[4]

They also founded new towns such as Baldock in Hertfordshire, replanned existing settlements as at Witham in Essex, and undertook rebuilding at Carcassone in the Faubourg de St Vincent.[5] Licences to hold markets and fairs not only in towns but in more rural areas added to the Templars' income. Noble overlords granted them other rights, such as the right to hold local courts, and the tithes and advowsons or livings of churches.

Litigation during the thirteenth century shows that the Templars were jealous of their rights over property and would challenge anyone daring to impinge on these in the courts. But they were not above impeding access and moving fences to impinge on the property of others.[6]

The widespread and disparate Templar estates were farmed with the objective of sending at least one-third of produce or profits east. On some estates the original grant laid down that all the products or profits should be sent to the Holy Land. John Harcourt's grant to the Templars of the manor and soke of Rothley in Leicestershire for example stipulated this.[7] Overall, until near the end of the thirteenth century the Templars were good landlords and productive farmers. But by the end of the thirteenth century there is evidence that managing all their resources in the West was becoming a burden. They were overstretched, and in England at least by the early fourteenth century some of their property was in need of repair and the land was derelict.

The Knights Templar in France

As might be expected from an order founded by a Frenchman, the Knights Templar had vast estates in France (Map 5.1). These were concentrated in the south and west, with a quarter of the French Templar houses being in the mountainous and isolated region of the Auvergne.[8] They had 53 commanderies in the Languedoc and south-west France, including urban houses in Toulouse, Carcassonne, Narbonne, Orange, Avignon, Nîmes, Aix and Marseilles.[9] It was vital that the Templars maintained a foothold in this area as it was close to the shipping route to the East, and from here produce, men and livestock could be despatched. It was an area of sea surrounded by mountains, which became a refuge for those who sought shelter, and this was a region embued with heresy and the subject of a deadly and bitter crusade by the Catholic armies against the heretics.

However, as well as commanderies in the south of France they had 18 commanderies in Normandy.[10] Studies of the rural commanderies in France show these to have been working farms each with its own chapel. There was some specialization, for example a stud farm at Richerenches and vineyards where appropriate, and cheese-making at Roquefort. Often the farms were fortified, but the 1307 inventories show that the interiors were fairly comfortable with soft furnishings, and the commandery chapels were often richly decorated. Unlike inventories from elsewhere, French inventories show that there were stores of arms kept in rural Templar houses, including helmets and crossbows.[11] The Templars in France planned a number of new villages and areas of towns, and Templar

MAP 5.1 ◆ *Templar sites in France*

property in towns was marked with a cross. A rare obit role from Rheims shows them to be fully integrated into the local community.[12]

Helen Nicholson points out that the Templars would have been familiar figures in the local community.[13] In fact they must have stood out with their long beards, short hair and distinctive white or black mantles endorsed with the crusader crosses. Unlike most other religious orders they did not stay in their houses but travelled around. Most Templars attended the annual provincial chapter, and there is evidence from safe-conducts issued by the Crown of a continual flow of Templars between

Britain and Europe. For example, Jacques de Molay the last Grand Master visited England. Each provincial master was expected to visit the East at least once every five years. Thus William de la More, the last English master, was given permission by Edward I to travel to Cyprus.

The Templars as bankers to the nobility and officers of state

Had they been content to remain as farmers and landlords perhaps the Templars in the West might not have attracted so much attention. But these were men from a section of society trained to and accustomed to rule. In the East they were expected to advise princes on policies and military strategy. In the West they held high positions in the courts of England, France and Iberia.

The Templars operated their own pilgrim tours from Marseilles to the East, and they had their own fleet. The nucleus of the 'royal' navy in England founded by King John was a second-hand ship purchased from the Templars, costing £133. In the 1220s Brother Thomas of the Templars oversaw the building of a 'great ship' at Portsmouth and in 1226 organized a muster of 200 ships for the king.[14] In England and France they acted as royal treasurers, bankers and trustees for the nobility. They operated a system of safe-deposit boxes and current accounts, as well as providing a courier service taking money from one part of Europe to another. They were able to do this because they had a network of safe houses across Europe where they could stay, and exchange money into the appropriate currency.

One of the functions performed by the Templars was the collection of royal and papal taxes. Once collected the money was taken to a Templar stronghold such as the Paris or London Temple to be counted and conveyed to the royal exchequer or to the pope. The money was transported in carts with an armed guard, and it must have been the sight of the cash going into the Temple that gave rise to the belief that the Templars were fabulously wealthy. As the Templars themselves were exempted from most taxes and tithes this helped to make them doubly unpopular. The Saladin tithe of 1188 demanded 10 per cent of income and movable goods from everyone except those exempt. It raised £70,000 in England. This was a very unpopular tax. It seemed as if these ancillary roles in the

West, as the counsellors of kings, as bankers and as tax collectors, perverted the Templars' original aim of protecting the Holy Land and broke the Templars' vow of poverty.

Until the end of the thirteenth century, maintaining a presence in the Holy Land was the Templar's main concern, and the policy of the Grand Masters, especially Jacques de Molay, was geared to this. But a change had come across the Order by the later years of the century. Members now existed who had never been East, and who were better administrators than they were fighters, and there were provincial masters who became embroiled in local politics, which led to the spilling of Christian blood. There grew up a division, albeit an almost invisible one, between the commanderies in the West and those clinging onto a presence in the Holy Land.

The world was changing, and the Templars needed to change with it. They failed to do this, with disastrous consequences.

Notes

1 Marquis D'Albon, *Cartulaire générale de l'Ordre du Temple*, Paris: Librairie Ancieune Honoré Champion (1913), pp. 12–13, 21, 30, 40.

2 E. Lord, 'The Knights Templar in Hertfordshire: Farmers and Landlords', *Herts Past & Present*, 3rd series, issue 6, (Autumn 2005), pp. 3–11.

3 B. Lees, (ed.), *The Records of the Templars in England in the Twelfth Century*, London: British Academy, Records of Economic and Social History of England. IX (1935).

4 P. Gerard, and E. Magnon; *Cartulaire des Templier De Douzens,* Paris: Bibliotheque Nationale (1965), pp. xxiv, xxx.

5 Gerard and Magnon, p. xxix.

6 It is unfortunate that much of what we know about the way in which the Templars managed their estates comes from two ends of the spectrum: inventories taken in the twelfth century, and inventories taken when the Templars were arrested. We also have the accounts of the commissioners put in to run the estates whilst the Templars were on trial, but we do not know whether they managed them in the same way as the Templars had. Litigation provides another element, but what is missing are the manorial accounts and manorial court records.

7 T.H. Fosbrooke, 'Rothley – the Preceptory', *Leicestershire Archaeological Society Transactions* (1921–2), pp. 2–32.

8 R. Sève and A.M. Chagny-Sève, *Le Procès des Templiers d'Auvergne*, Paris: Editions du C.T.H.S. (1986), 25.

9 D. Selwood, *Knights of the Cloister Templars and Hospitallers in Central-Southern Occitan c1100–c1300*, Woodbridge: Boydell Press (1999), p. 1.

10 M. Miguet, *Templiers et Hospitaliers en Normandie*, Paris: CTHS (1995), 15.

11 Selwood, pp. 29, 200–1.

12 *Obitarium Templi Remensis*, Melanges historiques Collection des documents inedits, vol. IV (1882).

13 H. Nicholson, *The Knights Templar: A New History* Gloucester: Alan Sutton (2002), p. 5.

14 *Calendar of Patent Rolls*, ed. T. Hardy, HMSO: *Rotuli Literarum Clausum de Turri Londonensis*, (1903[1844]), London: George Eyre, vol. 2, pp. 14, 39,62,94,113–4,122, 160, 167,194.

CHAPTER 6

· · · · · · · · · · · · · · · ·

The fall of Acre and the doomed man

L ouis IX left the East in April 1254 having been ransomed from prison by money provided by the Knights Templar. Eastern Christendom was being threatened by the Mamelukes in Egypt and the Mongols. This threat stopped the squabbling between the military orders and a truce was agreed. Letters and envoys were sent west pleading for help.

In June 1258 a Templar envoy arrived in London. He had covered the distance from the East in a mere 13 weeks. He brought dire news that the Mongols were devastating the Holy Land, and that the Christians were powerless to stop them, as they used Christian prisoners as a human shield in front of their armies. The military orders were being annihilated.[1] Weakened by their conflict with the Mongols the Templars withdrew to their castles. This was an opportunity for others to strike. One by one the Baybars and the Mamelukes took the Templar strongholds: Safed, Beaufort, Baghras all fell. Desperately the Templars fortified the castles they still held. But the problem of manpower recurred; they did not have enough men to hold their castles for long.

The castle at Atlit appeared to be impregnable. In July 1266 Baybars tried three times to take it, but it stood firm. Eventually, it was betrayed by one of its occupants, a Syrian Christian who negotiated a safe-conduct. When the gates were opened the women and children were captured and sold into slavery, and the surviving Templars decapitated. The loss of Atlit was a disaster. It guarded the route to Acre, Tyre and Sidon, and without its protection movement became difficult. It looked as though the

Christians would be forced to leave the Holy Land, but as we have seen respite came with another crusade initiated by Louis IX in 1269 and taken over by his brother Charles of Anjou after Louis's death in 1270. Charles, whose real ambitions were in Europe, withdrew in November 1270, having achieved very little. But he was followed into the field by a charismatic Englishman, the Lord Edward (later Edward I), eldest son of Henry III. Although, like Charles, Edward achieved little, his presence helped to pull the Christian army together and achieve some stability. Edward was able to negotiate a ten-year treaty with Baybars, which would give the Christians time to retrench and for the military orders to regroup and recruit new members.

It was too late. The crusader states were fatally weakened, and rent by internal divisions. A call by Pope Gregory in 1274 for a new crusade fell on deaf ears in the West. There were other ways available to gain absolution and remission from Purgatory that did not involve the discomfort and danger of military service in a desert land. The penitent could join a guild and through this have masses said for his soul to speed his way through purgatory.[2] No leader emerged to take up the pope's appeal. Edward of England was busy conquering Wales and Scotland. Charles of Anjou was involved in pursuing his dynastic ambitions in Sicily.

Christians fighting Christians in the East: Grand Master William Beaujeu's policies

Charles' dynastic ambitions were to spill out into the East and complicate matters there when Maria of Antioch sold her claim to the Kingdom of Jerusalem to him, despite the fact that Hugh III of Cyprus had already been enthroned in Tyre. The Templars supported Charles's claim. He was a member of the ruling house of France where they had a great deal of property and political influence; a great many of the Order's members had a French origin; and William of Beaujeu, elected Grand Master of the Order in 1273, was distantly related to Charles. Malcolm Barber suggests that he was Charles' candidate for the post of Grand Master.[3] The Templar of Tyre, who became Beaujeu's secretary, describes him as a 'gentle man' and suggests that he was also related to Louis de Beaujeu the constable of France.[4]

Although elected in 1273 Beaujeu spent the first two years of his grand mastership in Europe, amassing resources to continue the fight in the East, and advising the pope on how to proceed in sponsoring a crusade. Beaujeu arrived in Acre in September 1275; once there his loyalty to Charles became obvious, and the Templars became open supporters of the Angevin cause. Beaujeu took the Order far away from the ideal of Hugh de Payens, its first Grand Master. He involved the Templars in a civil war in Tripoli that led to the spilling of Christian blood, forbidden by the Rule and by St Bernard. Western-style politics had intruded into and perverted the Order.

It is clear, however, that Beaujeu wanted at all costs to preserve the Order and its position in the Holy Land. Where necessary he made treaties with the Muslims in the realization that unless help arrived from the West all they could do was to hang on and survive in a hostile world. In 1282 a truce was signed between Beaujeu and Lord al-Malik Qalawun in Acre. A peace was to last for ten years from 15 April 1282. It applied to Egypt, with its provinces, borders and ports, to Syria with its districts, castles, fortresses and ports, and to Tortosa held by the Order of the Temple and to their lands recognized in perpetuity. Tortosa was not to be fortified and the safety of the sultan's subjects was to be guaranteed. The sultan undertook not to attack by sea but if one of his ships was wrecked on the coast at Acre then the Templars agreed to aid the survivors, and the Sultan would aid Christian survivors wrecked on his coast.[5] This policy was misunderstood in the West and also by members of the Order. It appeared that the Knights Templar were consorting with the enemy, and they were accused of adopting Islamic ways. Yet even Pope Gregory IX agreed to an alliance with the Mongols in an attempt to stem the tide of the Mamelukes, though to no avail, as rivalry between the military orders and dynastic struggles had terminally weakened the Christian forces. Moreover more rivalry had developed between the Genoese, Venetians and Pisans settled in the Holy Land, with the Templars supporting the Venetians.

In Acre fighting broke out between the supporters of Bohemond III and Guy of Gibelet. The Templars supported Guy, and Bohemond retaliated by attacking their house in Tripoli in 1283, using Muslim mercenaries. A truce lasting a year was negotiated, but in 1284 Beaujeu attacked Bohemond's possessions in the County of Tripoli and finally, with the help of Guy of Gibelet, Tripoli itself. Guy's spies inside the city promised to open the gate but they failed to do this; the Templars then withdrew their support from him, he surrendered and was executed. It may have been politic for the Templars to withdraw from Tripoli and prevent further loss to the Order, but it was seen as an act of treachery against those who had counted them as their friends.

What could be described either as further treachery or as good strategy can be seen when the Templars abandoned their support for Charles of Anjou and encouraged Henry II of Cyprus to enter Acre in 1286. A year later Western politics again intervened in the East when war broke out between the Italian city-states of Pisa and Genoa. The Venetians, who supported the Pisans, had a strong presence in Acre, which encouraged the Genoese to attack the city. The military orders tried to intervene between the warring Italian states whose squabbles had permeated the East, and eventually it was agreed that the Genoese would have Tripoli as their naval base. This threatened the sultan of Egypt who began to arm his troops against the Genoese. Tripoli was under siege by 25 March 1287 and the city fell on 27 April 1287. The population were massacred or sold into slavery and the city destroyed. Acre would be the Sultan's next destination.

On 12 February 1290 Pope Nicholas IV proclaimed a new crusade with the avowed aim of freeing the Holy Land from Islam and placing it firmly under Christian rule. Any hope of success was lost by Christian treachery. James II of Aragon and the king of Sicily made a truce with the sultan of Egypt that they would not support the crusade providing their subjects could have safe passage to go on pilgrimage to Jerusalem. The Genoese also entered into a truce with the sultan, partly out of pique because the Venetians were supporting the crusade.

The crusaders left for the Holy Land at Easter 1290, and took up position at Acre. In August 1290 they violated the treaty made by the herd Edward, new Edward I, and attacked a caravan. This was the excuse the sultan had been waiting for. He demanded that those responsible be handed over to him for punishment. Whether the Templars had been involved in the attack is not known, but it was the Grand Master William of Beaujeu who advised calling the sultan's bluff and sending him the occupants of Acre gaol instead of the crusaders. His advice was not taken, and it was seen by the crusaders as agreeing to the sultan's demands, and therefore a dishonourable course of action.

The Sultan was now ready to attack.

The Siege of Acre

On 1 May 1291 an army of 70,000 horsemen and 150,000 foot soldiers arrived beneath the walls of Acre. Acre was a fortified city, and the Templars had a fortified citadel within it on a corniche on the coastal side of the city. The citadel could be defended when the rest of the city fell, and access to the sea meant that escape was possible, and in the last desperate days of the siege refugees poured into the Templar compound. On 4 May the sultan brought up two gigantic *mangonels*, siege engines designed to throw projectile at castle walls and breach them. He also sent in engineers to undermine the walls. He offered Henry II of Cyprus the chance to evacuate the civilian population. Henry refused. Defenders tried to disable the siege engines in a sortie beyond the walls led by William Beaujeu. They failed and were beaten back. The siege continued until 15 May when the sultan's engineers succeeded in collapsing the New Tower. Preparations were made for evacuating women and children by sea through the Templars' compound, but a heavy storm prevented this.

The assault started on the following day. The Templar of Tyre who was present in Acre described how the Saracens assaulted Acre on all sides, and having got through the first walls and ditches, approached the Barbican and entered by the great tower called the Accursed Tower. They won through to St Romano where the Pisans had their engines, whilst the others came in on the road by the St Antoine Gate.

> The master of the Temple with 10 or 12 brothers set out to defend the St Antoine Gate which lay between the two walls and passed the Guard of the Hospital and were joined by the Master of the Hospital. And when the two masters of the Temple and the Hospital came they found one wall breached and alight, and archers firing arrows through the fire.[6]

There was fighting in the streets of Acre as the Templars and Hospitallers tried to defend the port area so that the civilian population could escape. It was during this street fighting that William de Beaujeu was mortally wounded, and carried back to the Templars' compound. The Templars were now leaderless. The defenders of the Accursed Tower and the inner walls withdrew.

The city fell on 19 May, but the Templar citadel held out under the command of Peter de Sevry, the Order's marshal. If he could hold onto the citadel there was still hope for those left in the city. On 25 May the sultan agreed that the civilian population could leave, but he had no control over his soldiers. The occupants of religious houses, Dominicans, Franciscans, monks and nuns were slaughtered and their chapels violated. Three days later the sultan forced those in the great tower (the Templar keep) to surrender. The Knights Templar submitted to the last man, and to the last man they were decapitated outside the city walls.[7]

The city was razed to the ground, and those who remained were sold into slavery. The last cities and castles in crusader hands began to fall like nine pins: Tyre and Beirut also in May, Sidon in July, Tortosa and the final foothold, the castle of Athlit, in August.

The Knights Templar leave the Holy Land

The Templars were expelled from the Holy Land and it was lost to the Christians. Some Templars had managed to escape by sea from Acre: Thibaut Gaudin left carrying the Templar treasure and their archives; Jacques de Molay also survived. He had repudiated Beaujeu's policy of appeasement, and now followed Gaudin and led a little band of survivors to Cyprus.

When they arrived in Cyprus, these wounded and exhausted survivors of the battle for Acre, they had no Grand Master to direct them. They needed a leader quickly, and it seems that Thibaut Gaudin was elected – or at least put forward as worthy of the task. He was a long-time member of the Order with a great deal of experience of fighting in the East. If he was elected, as some sources suggest, then the pope as overall commander of the Order should have been informed. There is no record of him having been notified, but in the shock waves that followed the Christian withdrawal from the Holy Land such detail may have been omitted. Gaudin died a year later in 1292, leaving the position of Grand Master vacant once more.

The election of Jacques de Molay as Grand Master

According to witnesses at the trial of the Templars there were now two candidates for the post of Grand Master: Jacques de Molay and Hugues de

Pairaud, the master of the Auvergne. De Pairaud had no experience in the East, but the focus of the Order had changed. It was their Western possessions that were important now. These gave them revenues and power, and access to the ears of princes and prelates who might be persuaded to launch a new crusade. Furthermore, de Pairaud was well connected in the Order, since many of his relations had held high office within it. But he had no plan for the re-conquest of the Holy Land. His policy was one of acting as a servant to the Crown and adjusting to the circumstances of the day even if this meant losing the Order's autonomy. De Molay was the complete opposite. He was a soldier and a man of action who had fought in countless campaigns in the East. He valued the Order's independence and its loyalty to the pope rather than to secular princes, and was vehemently opposed to any infringement of the Order's rights. Alain Demurger describes de Pairaud as the modernist, de Molay as the reactionary.[8] It could be added that de Pairaud was the diplomat and man of letters, de Molay the plainspoken soldier who lacked the guile to dissemble when needed. He was an unfortunate choice, however, as the Order needed a modern man like de Pairaud to lead it through the changes to come. De Pairaud had the ear of the French king, and it was de Pairaud who supported the French king in his quarrel with Pope Boniface VIII.

De Molay's outlook was conservative, and this might have contributed to the Order's downfall. On the other hand he had a missionary zeal in the cause of regaining and holding the Holy Land for the Christians, and maintaining the Order as a Christian fighting force. Was this what the Order wanted? De Molay was elected, but it is not clear whether majority supported him. After the event it was claimed that it had been a corrupt election, and that the French Templar chapters had disagreed with the outcome.

After his election de Molay came west to visit the Order's European houses. He visited England, France, Italy and Aragon, on a mission to elicit help for a new crusade. In the event he returned to Cyprus in 1296 without any firm promise of action. Since 1291 Cyprus had been the Order's headquarters. It was ideally placed to launch an invasion of Palestine, and it provided a rallying place for Western forces to gather and for resources to be stored. The Templars had five commanderies on the island at Akrotirie, Famagusta, Limassol, Nicosia and Paphos, together with four castles, and there were probably more Templar Knights on Cyprus than elsewhere.

De Molay's visit to the West had not produced the desired effect, but together with the king of Cyprus and the Hospitallers he sailed for Egypt in 1300. The combined force took Tortosa, and the Templars occupied the island of Ruad until 1302 when they were expelled.

In Cyprus de Molay meddled with island politics, supporting the coup in 1306 that deposed Henry II. Later in that year de Molay was summoned west by the pope who wanted his advice on a new campaign in the East, and his thoughts on the unification of the Knights Templar and the Knights Hospitaller. De Molay would never return to Cyprus.

This lengthy story of the Templars' exploits up to the time that de Molay left Cyprus for the last time has served two purposes. One is to show that the Knights Templar died in their hundreds for what they believed. Their bravery was legendary and commented on by Christian and Arabs alike. The knight with the red cross on his mantle became the symbol of chivalry and all that was good in humankind. He was incorporated into legends and romances.

The other purpose has been to show that even before the fourteenth century the unpopularity of the Knights Templar was growing. Part of this stemmed from economic factors. The Templars did not pay tithes and taxes, and the Order were assumed to be fabulously rich. As collectors of other people's taxes they were doubly damned. Commentators saw them as arrogant, disobedient and lacking in humility. William of Tyre was not afraid to write this, and to suggest that they were more interested in booty than winning the war for the Christians.

At Damascus in 1149 they were accused of taking a bribe to give bad advice which forced the Christian army to withdraw. In 1153 at Ascalon they were accused of greed and deceit. The defeat at the Horns of Hattin in 1189 was blamed on them. They were alleged to be oppressive landlords in Cyprus in 1199. Their rivalry with the other military orders was seen as weakening the Christian effort in the Holy Land. Their stiff-necked code of honour was said to have contributed to the defeat at Mansurah. They were accused of meddling in politics and giving bad counsel. Pope Innocent III suggested that they used the cloak of religion for worldly gain, and in 1223 Pope Honorius III's bull *De insolata templarium* was a reprimand to the English Templars for abusing their privileges, usurping others' domains, preventing customary dues to the king, disregarding manorial customs, and engaging in vexatious law.

Among the less exalted folk, there were scurrilous rhymes and sayings about the Templars: for example, a drunkard was said to drink like a Templar, a blasphemer to swear like a Templar, and it was said that no girl became a woman until she had slept with a Templar. The sobriquet for a brothel in German was 'Tempelhaus'. None of which helped the Templars' reputation, but neither do they represent the charges actually made against them in 1307.

In 1306 the pope asked de Molay and the master of the Hospitallers to compile memoranda on what was needed to start a new crusade, and to explain why the two orders should not be merged. This was not the first time that a merger had been suggested. It was discussed in 1274 at the Council of Lyons and again in 1291 and dismissed on both occasions, and the Canterbury Council of 1291 suggested, along similar lines, that funding for another crusade should come from the possessions of the Templars and Hospitallers.

Only the first part of the memorandum of the master of the Hospitallers has survived. Like de Molay he thought that the pope should lead the crusade, and he suggested that the First Crusade should be used as a model of how to proceed. The pope should preach a crusade and raise a special tax to fund it. These funds should be used to buy mercenary help as well as helping those who had taken the cross. All participants in the crusade were to be under the protection of the Church and to be offered absolution. He followed de Molay's idea that the crossing should be in secret. The portion of the document that is the Hospitallers' response to the suggestion that the two orders should merge is missing.

The full text of de Molay's memorandum has survived. He started by stating his ideas on the conduct of a new crusade. It should be led by the pope himself, and all western troops should muster and cross to the Holy Land in one sailing, but to go to a secret destination known only to de Molay himself. He would inform the pope of that destination once they had set sail. The fleet in which they would sail should be chartered from the Italian republics. They would need at least 12,000 horsemen and 5,000 foot soldiers to have any chance of success. He asked that galleys be sent to protect Cyprus and that any Christians who did business with the enemy should be punished.

De Molay drew up a list of pros and cons on the question of whether the Orders should be merged (see Table 6.1). The pros were practical and

TABLE 6.1 ◆ *De Molays list of pros and cons*

Pros (for the merger)	Cons (against the merger)
A large merged order would offer protection from their critics.	It might be dangerous to force two ancient orders together.
A merger would help the finances of both Orders.	Competition was beneficial both in the field and in encouraging gifts.
It would strengthen both Orders in a number of respects.	The new Rule would be a compromise between the strict Templar and the less stringent Hospitallers.
It would reduce operating costs.	A merger would result in the closure of some Templar and Hospitaller houses and chapels.
	It would cause discontent and bitterness.
	Offices would have to be amalgamated causing friction.[9]

actually gave excellent reasons for merging the orders. The cons are much more specious and it is clear that de Molay found it difficult to justify his rejection of an amalgamated order. He ended by saying that he was willing to give counsel, but the pope must make up his own mind. This raises the interesting question as to what de Molay would have done had the pope insisted on a merger. Would he have broken away from papal control and turned the Templars into an autonomous body with no responsibility to Church or State? Would the Templars and de Molay have survived if he had agreed to a merger? We must also ask whether de Molay was aware that the political situation in Europe had changed. His nemesis Philip IV of France was challenging the papacy, and a merged order might well have come under his control. But Philip was a man adept at hiding his actual intentions, and when de Molay stepped ashore in France in December 1306 he had no idea what would happen.

He was a doomed man.

Notes

1   Matthew Paris, *Flores Historium*, ed. H.R. Luard, London: HMSO (1890), pp. 451–2.

2 Women could also join guilds, but in this instance it refers to men who might have gone on crusade.

3 M. Barber, *The New Knighthood*, Cambridge: Cambridge University Press (1994), p. 169.

4 *Chronique du Templier de Tyr, 1424–1309* in *Les Gestes des Chiprois* (1887) ed. G. Raynaud, p. 218.

5 F. Gabrielli, trans., *Arab Historians of the Crusades*, London: Routledge (1984), pp. 323–5, 330–1.

6 Raynaud, p. 248.

7 Gabrielli, p. 346.

8 A. Demurger, *The Last Templar* trans. A. Nevill, London: Profile Books (2004), pp. 68–70.

9 G. Lizerand, *Le Dossier des Templiers*, Paris: Librairie Ancienne Honore Champion (1923), pp. 2–15.

CHAPTER 7

Rumours and arrests

Jacques de Molay in France

Jacques de Molay landed in France in November 1306. He then disappears from the records until May 1307. He may have travelled to Aragon to discuss events there, or toured the southern French houses. By that time he probably knew that there were rumours abroad about the Knights Templar, but may have thought that these were relatively harmless, merely reviving the old chestnuts of pride, arrogance and lack of charity.

De Molay's lack of political acumen may have meant that he was unaware of the tensions in France between the king and the pope, and did not understand the true character and ambitions of Philip IV, king of France. The Templars were caught in the crossfire in a conflict of which they do not seem to have been fully aware. They naturally looked to the pope for his support as their overall commander, believing that no harm could come to the Order if he was behind them. De Molay's rival for the Grand Master's post, Hugues de Pairaud, already had Philip's ear, and would therefore be in a better position to mediate with the king on behalf of the Order. Moreover he had already supported Philip over the business of Pope Boniface.

Philip IV of France

Much of what happened later hinged on the characters of the three main protagonists, Philip IV of France, Pope Clement V and Jacques de Molay.

Philip IV, sometimes called Philip the Fair, had an overwhelming ambition to unite the provinces of France under his central rule, and to gather all power into his hands. He was the first French king to levy national taxes, and he created a central bureaucracy around himself to carry out his orders. His critics described him as handsome but empty, but his good looks in themselves made him a potent symbol of the monarchy in France, and indeed of France itself. He was born in about 1266, the second son of Philip III and Isabella of Aragon. His elder brother died in 1276 leaving him heir to the throne. In 1284 he married Jeanne of Navarre, the heiress to the fiefs of Champagne and Navarre. This marriage brought into Crown hands these fiefs, which thus became part of France as a nation-state. Only Aquitaine, Brittainy, Burgundy and Flanders remained outside his grasp. He tried to impose French rule on these regions but was heavily defeated in Flanders, and had to go to war with England over Aquitaine.

Philip ascended the throne a year after his marriage, in 1285. As King of France he was also described as the vicar of God, and was anointed with oil allegedly sent down from heaven. As a representative of God on earth any opposition to him was seen not only as treason, but as sacrilege and heresy as well. He took the role of king very seriously. He was personally pious and publicly was known as a persecutor of heretics and those he saw as opposing the Catholic Church. It was in this role that he accused Pope Boniface VIII of heresy and immorality, seeing it as his duty as a Christian monarch to act against him. But it was not only religion that was involved. As in so many of Philip's actions there were layers beneath the surface. Boniface had opposed Philip's taxes and had threatened to join with the king of England, who had complained about Philip to him, and there had also been disagreements about who could appoint clerics in France. Thus there were political and financial nuances in Philip's persecution of Boniface.

The persecution of Boniface by Philip has some similarities with his persecution of the Templars. It started with rumours being put abroad about Boniface's religious beliefs and his personal life. On 12 June 1303 at a general assembly in Paris, Philip accused Boniface of heresy, sodomy and simony, all charges he was eventually to level at the Templars. On 8 September, with the agreement of the national assembly – thus adding a spurious legality to his actions – Philip sent his chief minister Guillaume de Nogaret to arrest Boniface. Nogaret forced his way into Boniface's palace at Anagni. But on 9 September the people of Anagni drove Nogaret out and rescued Boniface, sending him to Rome under an armed guard. This was a clear indication of what Philip could do to those who opposed him, or got in his way. On 11 October 1303 Boniface died. His successor Benedict XI was elected in November and immediately absolved Philip IV of his sin in accusing Boniface.[1]

Despite his taxation schemes Philip was chronically hard up. The treasury was depleted by his wars against Flanders and England, and by the of the enormous bureaucracy he had founded. In 1306 the Jews were expelled from France and their assets seized, and this was followed by the expulsion of the Lombard bankers and the seizure of their property.

It was economics that had brought Philip and the Knights Templar together. The royal house of France used the Templars as their bankers, and although they were removed from this role at various times, the French kings were unable to find a satisfactory replacement and usually returned to the Templars. The accounts held by the Templars were carefully audited with no hint of complicity or desire to swindle Philip. The Templars frequently lent him money, and by 1307 he was 260,000 *livres parisi* in debt to them. He had, therefore a financial reason for wanting to get rid of the Templars, to cancel out his debts, and take over their assets. In order to do this he needed the acquiescence of the new pope, Clement V.

Pope Clement V

Clement had started life as Bertrand Got. He came from a good family who had already supplied the Church with several leading clerics. He started his career by reading canon law at the universities of Orleans and Bologna, and rose quickly in the Church, becoming Archbishop of Bordeaux in 1299. After the death of Benedict IX the College of Cardinals had not been able to agree on a successor. The Italians wanted an Italian pope, the French a French pope, and the French were supported by Philip IV who threatened to revive accusations of Boniface's heresy. Only a strong pope would be able to keep Philip in check, but Clement was Philip's candidate, and when he was elected it was soon obvious that instead Philip was going to control him.

Clement's first encyclical included a section on the recovery of the Holy Land. But he soon found that Philip IV's support did not come without strings. Clement had to publicly denounce Boniface's memory and appoint cardinals who were favourable to France. Worse still, Clement forsook Italy for the Dominican priory at Avignon, breaking the old tradition that the pope lived in or near St Peter's city of Rome. The Italians condemned him for leaving Italy, and accused him of simony, avarice, nepotism and immorality. French lawyers tried to justify the move, suggesting that the move to Avignon was a move to seek absolution for the sins of Boniface. The truth was that the climate at Avignon suited Clement's health better than that of Rome.

Was Clement completely under Philip's thumb? He had the terrible example of what Philip had done to Boniface before him to keep him in line. Left to himself he would probably be known as a good administrator who encouraged learning. But with Philip breathing down his neck he did not stand a chance. He owed his position to Philip and if he opposed him Philip could break him.

Jacques de Molay

The third protagonist in this final act of the Knights Templar was Jacques de Molay, another Frenchman, who may have come from the Haut Saone. He was probably born between 1244 and 1247. Nothing is known of his family and whether he came from a Templar family, but we know it must have been a knightly family. He entered the Order at Beaune in 1265, his initiation being overseen by Brother Humbert de Pairaud, knight, in the presence of Aumary de la Roche and many others.[2] He was in the East by the early 1270s, and was one of a group of younger knights who were frustrated by William de Beaujeu's policy of appeasement and truce. They wanted to prove themselves in the field. He fought valiantly at the siege of Acre and was one of the band of knights who escaped to Cyprus. When elected as Grand Master his main aim was to regain a footing in the Holy Land.

He described himself as unlettered and uneducated and he clearly found it difficult to dissemble. Unfortunately, most of what we know about him comes from the trial process, and this does not show him in the best light. Other information comes from the anonymous Templar of

Tyre who had been William de Beaujeu's secretary and was biased against de Molay. He described him as a mean and avaricious man. De Molay's early confession, whether obtained by torture or not, suggests certain cowardice under pressure. His subsequent behaviour in first refusing to defend the Order, and then making a poor fist of it, shows him to be confused. It is only with his retraction and death at the stake that the true spirit of the man emerges, and this leads to the question of what he was doing in the years leading up to the retraction. Was he playing a waiting game, confident that the pope would save the Order? Or did he simply not know what to do? Here was a simple man caught between a ruthless prince and a pope who should have defended the Order but was unable to do so. The Templars' tragedy was also his personal tragedy. He was the wrong man in the wrong place at the wrong time.

Rumours about the Knights Templar

Even before de Molay landed in France in the winter of 1306 there were ugly rumours about the Order. These went beyond the usual accusation of avarice and pride, and hinted at strange practices that went on behind closed doors; of indecency at the initiation ceremony and the denial of Christ; the worship of idols alien to the Christian tradition. Where had these rumours originated? When examined in detail the rumours and the subsequent charges can be seen to be stock-in-trade accusations levelled at heretics in the fourteenth century. The denial of Christ, repudiation of the sacraments tinged with sorcery, and indecency were all charges levelled against the Albigensians and the Cathars in France. So it is possible that the original rumours were put about by Philip IV's agents.

These rumours appear to have taken hold and been accepted as fact sometime between 1305 and 1306. Various theories were put forward at the time as to how this happened. At his trial in 1309 Ponsard de Gizy named four traitors who were responsible for the Templars' troubles: Floyran de Bitteris, co-prior of Mont Agen, Bernard Pelet prior of the Mas d'Agen, a knight of the Agenais and a monk called William Robert.[3] But according to the Florentine chronicler Villani the rumours were based on a confession of a renegade Templar imprisoned in a royal castle who told a fellow prisoner, who in turn told Noffo Dei who recorded what was said. Amaury Augier claimed that the rumours came from

Esquieu de Floyran, and that de Floyran also got his information from a renegade Templar.[4]

The one name which keeps reappearing in these accounts is Esquieu or Esquin de Floyran. He first appears at the Aragonese court of James II where he repeated stories he had heard against the Templars. James II, who relied on the Templars for help to protect his borders against the Moors, did not believe him, and challenged him to verify the accusations, promising him a reward should he be able to do so. De Floyran cut his losses and moved on to France to seek an audience with Philip IV, who was all too ready to believe his accusations.

De Floyran told Philip that the Templars' loyalty to their Order was greater than their moral principles. He told how they spat on the cross, denied Christ, performed immoral acts and worshipped idols. They were, he told the French king, heretics, sodomites and sorcerers.[5] Was this the chance that Philip had been waiting for, or had he planned these revelations in advance? Let us pause to consider Philip's motives in wanting to get rid of the Templars.

First of all, there were political motives. Philip IV and the papacy were on a collision course. He had already accused one pope of heresy, and would have no compunction in getting rid of another. This was a power game in the raw: State versus the Church, secular power versus spiritual power. In attacking the Templars, by implication, Philip was attacking the pope who was their overall commander and their protector. It was an open insult to the papacy.

There were also financial reasons for Philip to dissolve the Order of Templars. He owed them a large amount of money, and was desperate for cash. The Templars owned many wealthy estates in France, the revenues from which would swell Philip's coffers nicely. Furthermore, the Templars were rumoured to be fabulously wealthy; wealth which Philip could use.

In addition there were personal reasons why Philip might have wanted to get rid of what he saw as a corrupt order. He was a deeply pious man, who wanted to lead a new crusade in which the military orders were united, a merger which Jacques de Molay refused to countenance. Philip had a superstitious fear of magic and evil spirits. The Templars were accused of idolatry, raising devils, worshipping idols, denying Christ, and dabbling with the occult; and Philip wanted to rid France of these abominations, and return it to a holy state. It seemed that the Templar ideal had failed, and as God's representative Philip wanted to set things right.[6]

De Molay appears to have had no idea how far things had gone when he arrived at the French court in the autumn of 1307. He was at first treated with the deference due to his rank, and given an audience with the king. On Thursday 12 October 1307 he acted as a pall-bearer at the funeral of Philip's sister-in-law Catherine of Valois. As far as he was concerned he was in Philip's favour and had nothing to fear.

The arrest of the Knights Templar in France

Philip had laid his plans carefully and discreetly. Secret orders had been issued to royal officials a month earlier on 14 September 1307, instructing them to arrest the Knights Templar

> on a matter too horrible to think about, too terrible to hear, a detestable crime, an abominable act, strange to all humanity. It has been reported by honourable persons that the Knights of the Temple are wolves who hide under the appearance of lambs in the habit of the order.[7]

On the day set aside for the arrests the royal officials were to be accompanied by good and honest men of the area, who were to be sworn to secrecy. Detailed inventories were to be taken of each commandery, and the arrested Templars were to be set under strong guard in isolation. The royal officials were empowered to use the threat of torture in order to extract confessions. The Templars were to be told that if they confessed they would be given a penance and absolved, if they did not they would be condemned to death. The arrests took place at dawn on Friday 13 October 1307. On that fateful morning there was complete confusion in the Templar houses across France as armed men broke down the doors and dragged the Templars from their beds and their prayers, shackled them in irons, and hauled them off to royal prisons. At this point the Templars did not know what charges were being made against them. Many of them were farmers rather than fighters, and had spent all their lives in rural commanderies in France, far from the battlefields of the East and the politics of Church and State. Most were taken completely by surprise. Some may have been forewarned, and a small number including Gerard de Villiers escaped before the arrests, allegedly taking the Templars' treasure with them. Others shaved their beards, threw off the Templar mantle and fled to the hills. Some managed to break away whilst the arrests were taking place. But on the whole everything was over by mid-morning of that Friday in October, and the majority of the French Templars were in prison. Most of them did not know why.

The arrests were a massive undertaking that must have involved a considerable number of men. That Philip IV could mobilize such a great force in secret is a tribute to his organizational skills. But what had he done? He, a secular prince, had acted against the greatest prince of the Church, the pope. The pope was the Templar Order's protector, and the Order was a religious order. Any charges against it should have been the business of the ecclesiastical courts, not a secular prince. Philip IV had thrown down a gauntlet against the pope and the Church. The Knights Templar were caught in the middle of a titanic struggle.

The Templar knights were shackled to walls in cold, dark dungeons, thick walls that muffled the screams of those being tortured in order to get them to confess. But to confess to what? As yet no charges had been brought against them. In fact the charges were to come from the confessions extracted by pain and deprivation, by the threat of eternal damnation to the fires of hell, and the withdrawal of all religious comforts. It did not take the torturers long to get what they wanted, and they got it from the best prize of all – Jacques de Molay.

Notes

1   J.R. Strayer, *The Reign of Philip the Fair*, Princeton: Princeton University Press (1980), pp. 277–82.

2   G. Lizerand, *Le Dossier de l'Affaire des Templiers*, Paris: Librairie Anciennne Honore Champion (1923), pp. 33–5.

3   J. Michelet, *Le Procès des Templiers*, Paris: Les Éditions du Comité des Travaux Historiques et Scientifiques (1987), vol. 1, pp. 36–7.

4   A. Demurger, *The Last Templar: The tragedy of Jacques de Molay Last Grand Master of the Temple*, trans. A. Nevill, London: Profile Books (2004), pp. 156–7.

5   E. Lord, *The Knights Templar in Britain*, London: Pearson Education (2004), pp. 239–40.

6   Lord, pp. 238–9.

7   Lizerand, pp. 16–19.

CHAPTER 8

· · · · · · · · · · · · · · ·

The French trial begins

De Molay's confession

The Templars reappeared in public a week after the arrests, when they were brought before a royal tribunal. At this point no charges had been given against them. The first Templar to appear on 21 October 1307 was Geoffrey de Charney, preceptor of Normandy, aged 56 years. He told the tribunal that he had been received into the Order at Etampes some 37–8 years earlier, by Amaury de la Roche and in the presence of Brother John le Fraunceys and others now dead. He described how the Templar mantle was placed round his neck and then a cross with the image of Christ on it was brought in and he was told that the image was of a false prophet who was not the son of God. He was told to spit upon the cross, but instead he spat upon the ground.

Asked about the kiss he was given at the initiation he said that he received a kiss on the navel from Amaury de la Roche. He had heard about the idol in the form of a head, and had heard Brother Gerard de Sauzet say that there were brothers who had kissed the head. He also explained that he had been told that now he was a Templar he must not debauch women, but must satisfy his desires with other brothers. He added that spitting on the cross and the profane kiss at the reception of new members of the order had since been discontinued, and that nothing against the Catholic Church was ever said or done in the Order. Asked if he had been tortured or threatened he replied 'No'.[1] Thus the very first witness from the Templars had condemned the Order.

Jacques de Molay, the Grand Master, was the next to appear before the tribunal on 24 October 1307.

Interrogation of Jacques de Molay October 24th 1307, the second year of the pontificate of Lord Clement V pope, and in the presence of religious men and brother William of Paris of the order of Preachers, inquisitor of the kingdom of France, by apostolic authority, in the house of the Knights Templar in Paris about the information against certain persons who have found themselves accused of the crime of heresy, in the presence of public notaries, brother Jacques de Molay Grand Master of the Order of the Knights of the Temple, swears before Holy God and the Saints Evangelical that what I am about to say is the truth pure and simple and entire, and questioned about the time and mode of his reception he said that was 42 years ago at Beaune in the diocese of Autun, by brother Humbert de Pairaud in the presence of brother Amuary de la Roche and many other brothers whose name I do not remember.

He said under oath that after he had promised to obey the rule the Order's mantle was put round his neck. A bronze cross with the image of Christ on it was produced and he was told to spit on it, but he spat on the floor. Asked about the point of chastity he said under oath that there was never any immodesty between brothers. Asked under oath if all the brothers were received in this way he said he thought that there were other ways. De Molay said he had not been tortured in order to make him confess.[2]

Hugues de Pairaud, de Molay's rival for the Grand Mastership, appeared before the Paris tribunal on 9 November 1307. His testimony was that he had been received into the Order at least 40 years ago, by his uncle Humbert. He had promised to obey the Order's Rule and to keep the Order's secrets. At the ceremony, the mantle was put around his neck, and he was then taken behind the altar where a cross with the image of Christ crucified on it stood. He was told to spit on this, not from the mouth but from the heart, and to deny Christ as a false prophet. When asked about the kisses he said he was kissed only on the mouth, but at other receptions he had observed he had seen the initiates kissed on the base of the spine. Most receptions included spitting on the cross and denying Christ, and those who refused were forced to do so by armed men.

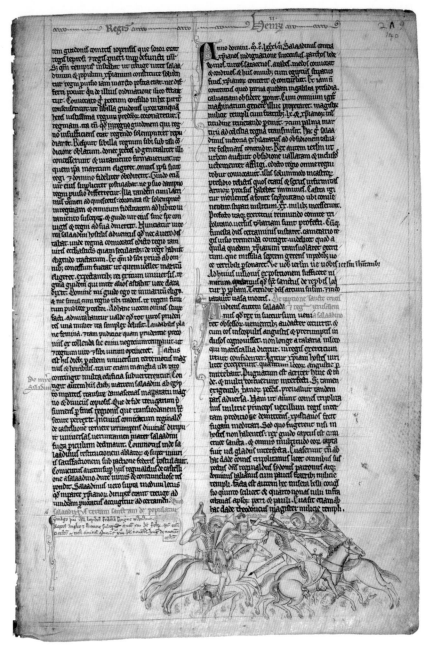

PLATE 1 ◆ The Battle of Hattin. Saladin seizing the True Cross from King Guy of Jerusalem, from Matthew Paris's *Chronica Majora*. In the picture the Saracens are distinguished by helmets with curlicues at the top, while the crusaders wear round helmets, and chain mail covered by a surcoat. Similar armour can be seen in the Winchester Bible of 1170, and the late-twelfth century *Life* of St Guthlac. Paris's work was written in the thirteenth century, but he may have consulted earlier sketches, and his friend Richard of Cornwall led a crusade and could have described Eastern battles and armour.

PLATE 2 ◆ The capture of Acre by Philip of France in 1191. The plate comes from the *Chronique de France*, compiled in the mid-fourteenth century. The besieging crusaders are wearing twelfth-century chain mail, though with fourteenth-century-style helmets similar to the Pembridge Helmet which belonged to Sir Richard Pembridge (d.1370). The Saracens defending Acre wear white turbans, which probably means they are civilians.

PLATE 3 ◆ *Tomb effigy of Philip IV of France in the Cathedral of St Denis, Paris*

PLATE 4 ◆ Jacques de Molay. This is an eighteenth-century realisation. There is no contemporary likeness of de Molay, but the beard here is an accurate depiction, though the Templars were advised to have short hair. The Latin inscription reads 'James of Burgundy, Last Master of the Templars Order' (de Molay was received into the order at Beaune in Burgundy).

PLATE 5 ◆ The Templars before Pope Clement and Philip IV of France. The pope sits higher than the king, as this is an ecclesiastical court. A cardinal adviser stands behind the pope and a lay adviser (possibly Guillaume de Nogaret) behind Philip. A layman ushers in the Templars, who wear brown robes, an indication that they are sergeants rather than knights.

Paris Temple Tower

PLATE 6 ◆ The Paris Temple. The Tower was originally part of a group of buildings enclosed within a wall, including a church and farms, a great hall where chapter meetings were held, a dungeon and a treasury. This is an artist's realisation of the Paris Temple tower, taken from a medieval manuscript, since the actual Temple was destroyed by Napoleon between 1805 and 1810.

PLATE 7 ◆ The London Temple. This shows the Round Nave of the London Temple church, completed in 1185. It was set within a monastic precinct, including cloisters, dormitories, the master's dwelling, farm buildings and a brewery. Outside the church little remains, apart from some medieval masonry in the west wall of the Inner Temple Hall.

PLATE 8 ◆ The burning of Jacques de Molay, from a fifteenth-century manuscript (part of the royal collection). The manuscript came into the hands of Richard of Gloucester (later Richard III) sometime between 1470 and 1483, and his autograph appears on folio 134. In the picture, the soldier shielding his face emphasises the agonising death he is witnessing. The bystanders are dressed in fifteenth-century apparel, including liripipe hats, tunics and hose similar to those seen in Memlinc's painting *The Mystic Marriage of St Catherine.* As well as being naked, De Molay and de Charney are close-shaven and tonsured, as members of a fifteenth-century religious order would have been, but the illustration is not necessarily an accurate portrayal of the burning.

He said under oath that they were told when they were received that it was permitted to have illicit relations with other brothers. Asked about the subject of the idol in the form of a head he said he had seen it under a cloth at Montpelier, and that all the brothers present had adored it. He said that the head had four feet, two behind and two in front of the face, and that the king's men had not found it when they arrested the Montpelier Templars. He said under oath that he had not been tortured.[3]

Thus the three most important Templars in France had confessed to participation in ceremonies where serious sins were committed, including denial of Christ, spitting on the cross, carnal kisses and relationships, and even worshipping an idol in the form of a head. In all 138 Templars examined by Guillaume de Paris in October and November 1307 confessed to some irregularities, and a further 94 made similar confessions at provincial tribunals.

However despite denials of torture, it was obvious that many of the brothers examined at the start of the trial had been racked or had flames applied to the soles of their feet. One was to appear before the papal commission with the bones of his feet in a bag. There is evidence in later examinations as to what had happened to them after their arrests. Sleep deprivation, solitary confinement shackled to a wall on a diet of bread and water were the mildest treatment they received. Gerard de Pasagio described how weights had been tied to him and he had been dropped from a great height.[4] This was the *strappado*, a means of torture used by the Inquisition. The victim's hands were bound and weights were tied to his feet and testicles. He was then hauled up to the ceiling and dropped. Bernard de Vado, a priest, described how fat was rubbed on his feet and these were held before a flame until he confessed. The bones of his feet dropped out as the flesh was burnt away. Peter Brocart, a farmer on the Templar estates in Paris, said he was stripped naked and tortured.[5] The mere threat of torture made some confess.

The Knights Templar and the University of Paris

On 25 October 1307 Jacques de Molay and other leading Templars were taken before members of the University of Paris to confess again. This further ordeal was imposed because Philip IV wanted to establish the legality of his actions and provide an intellectual rationale for them. It is probable that about this time de Molay sent a letter to the other Templars imprisoned in France ordering them to confess and be absolved, and avoid more torture and hardship. De Molay may have been sure that the pope would save them. But so far Clement had been able to do little.

When he received the news that Philip had arrested the Templars in France the pope was on his way to a consistory court at Poitiers. The arrests were a direct insult to him and the Church, and at a meeting held *in camera* on 15 October he decided, with the consent of the consistory court, to challenge Philip. At the same time he spoke to the Templars imprisoned at Poitiers, and told them not to despair as he was their traditional protector. On 22 November 1307 Clement issued a papal bull *Pastoralis praementiae*, which was designed to wrest the Templars from Philip and put them under the control of an ecclesiastical court. First the bull ordered all Christian princes to arrest the Templars in their lands and to take control of their property. As we shall see, other Christian princes were reluctant to do this when asked by Philip, but it was more difficult to disobey the pope who could excommunicate the prince and his country.

The bull mentioned rumours Clement had heard about the Templars and the free confession given by the Grand Master that confirmed the rumours. It promised that he, Clement, would pursue these matters and find out the truth.[6] Theoretically Philip IV handed over the Templars to Cardinals Fredol and de Suisy in December 1307. In practice no actual transfer took place, and some of those who had confessed began to retract their confessions, saying these had been extracted by force. In Poitiers the senior Templar under Clement's control, Olivier de Penne, preceptor of Lombardy, escaped from the unguarded house where Clement had placed him and disappeared. In order to show his good intentions to Philip, Clement offered a reward of 10,000 florins to anyone who could recapture de Penne.

Clement was now in a dubious position. He had openly criticized Philip IV and taken over the Templars' trial himself. But Philip had a greater force of arms, and Clement was virtually a prisoner at Poitiers.

Meanwhile in Paris Philip was anxious to tie up loose ends and establish the legality of his actions, since he had usurped papal power in arresting a religious order and accusing them of heresy, which was a purely ecclesiastical matter. In early 1308 he put a list of seven questions to the Masters of Theology of the University of Paris.

1. Should sacrilege be left to the church or could it be judged by a secular authority when there is relapse (referring to those Templars who had revoked their confessions)?

2. The Templars were a unique sect who through such horrible and abominable crimes had brought great peril to the temporal prince. They need to be extirpated. If the secular prince acts to do this is it deemed to be an act against the Church?

3. Five Templars from various regions of France have confessed. Does this condemn the whole Order?

4. Confessions made by various members of the Order have the ingredients of the occult. Can these brothers be received back into the Catholic Church?

5. Those who have confessed have done nothing but obey the Order's rules. Can they be condemned?

6. Can the secular prince confiscate the Templars' revenues for profit, or should these be sent to the Holy Land?

7. Have the Templars the right to these funds because they no longer protect the Holy Land?

The Masters of Theology at the University replied to these questions on 25 March 1308. They did not give the answers that Philip wanted but instead said that the Templars should be tried by the Church, and not the secular prince. This was followed by further consultation between Philip and other religious men from the University.[7] Philip was not ready to own himself beaten. In May 1308 he orchestrated a petition from the people of France deploring the scandals and heresy of the Knights Templar, and asking him to punish them for the good of the nation.

Neither had Philip finished coercing Clement V. On 29 May 1308 Guillaume de Plaisans was sent by Philip to address Clement in Poitiers, in rhetoric that was guaranteed to strengthen Clement's resolve against the Templars. He started his oratory by saying that the cross which was defiled by the Templars at their reception ceremony was the symbol of Christ's victory over death and redemption. The pope should punish any who defiled it and denounce the Templars. He pointed out that they had confessed their sins and declared themselves guilty. He asked Clement for swift justice and an end to the affair before the sins of the Templars corrupted the whole kingdom of France. If Clement did not act then all those who believed in the Christian faith would rise up and defend it. Clement must act or face the consequences of his vacillation.[8]

The French Templars were still in royal prisons. As a gesture of good will Philip sent 72 of them to Poitiers to testify to Clement between 29 June and 2 July 1308. These 72 had been hand-picked and they obediently repeated and embellished their confessions. They repeated the description of the Templar mantle being placed round their necks in a secret ceremony in which they had to deny Christ and spit on the cross. They added that they were given a cord to wear round their waist at all times, which had touched the idol. They described the idol in detail. They described the harsh punishments meted out for refusing to obey the Rule, homosexual acts, and the lack of charitable giving in Templar houses. They told Clement everything that Philip wanted him to hear. The majority of the 72 were sergeants or servants, and a number were apostates who had already fled from the Order. They were promised absolution provided they did not revoke their confessions, and having nothing to lose they agreed to this.

The result of hearing these confessions was that Clement agreed to open a papal inquisition on the matter of the Templars, but promised that in the meantime Philip could keep the revenues from their estates. So Philip had a positive result. So far no list of charges against the Templars had been drawn up, but this was done in August 1308 and was based on the confessions.

The Articles of Accusation against the Knights Templar

The Articles of Accusation fell into six categories:

1. Articles on reception into the Order:
   - Initiates were received in secret. At the reception they were told to spit on the cross and deny Christ as a false prophet who had not suffered on the cross for the sins of humanity and did not offer redemption.
   - At the reception indecent kisses were exchanged on the navel, buttocks, base of the spine and the penis.

- The initiate was given a cord that had touched an idol to wear at all times, and ordered to swear they would never leave the Order.
- Anyone who refused to do these things was killed or imprisoned.

2. Articles on idolatry:
   - Each province had its own idol, which was adored in the chapter meetings as god and saviour, and which was believed to give the Templars riches, and make the trees flower and the land germinate.
   - Some Templars worshipped a cat, others a head or a skull.
   - All Templars wore a cord that had touched an idol.

3. Articles on heresy:
   - The Templars denied Christ as a false prophet.
   - They did not believe in the sacraments or that the host was the body of Christ.
     If a Templar took mass in an outside church he averted his eyes when the host was raised.
   - The master, who was not an ordained priest, gave absolution.
   - Templars were permitted to confess to other brothers who were not priests.

4. Articles on immorality:
   - At the reception carnal kisses were exchanged.
   - The initiate was told that carnal relationships with other brothers were permitted and were not a sin.
   - Carnal relationships between brothers took place.

5. Articles on charity
   - The Templars did not offer hospitality as other religious houses did.
   - They did not consider it a sin to acquire property by illegal means.

6. Articles on secrecy
   - Chapter meetings took place in secret at night, behind locked and guarded doors, after all the servants had been sent away.[9]

These were the accusations that the papal inquisition was to put to the Templars when they took over the inquiry, and were based on the confessions of the 72 Templars sent by Philip to Clement. In a papal bull issued at the same time as the articles were drawn up Clement stated that he believed the accusations because he had heard the confessions for himself. He had heard that the Order was corrupt and was determined to make further inquiry into the accusations, and had appointed commissioners to go into the provinces on his behalf and search out the wrongdoers. The papal commissioners were told to concentrate on the corruption of the Order in general, and the corruption of individual members. It looked as though Philip IV had Clement in his pocket, and the process of investigating and condemning would be over quickly, with a satisfactory resolution for the King.

The papal inquisition

The Inquisition was founded by Pope Gregory IX in 1231; he gave the responsibility for operating it to the Dominican prior of Regensburg. The Dominicans could hear evidence and give judgement, and the whole process was legal. But as far as the Inquisition was concerned, dissident beliefs and heresy could mean whatever the papacy wanted condemned at the time. The Dominicans were trained to identify heretics by their custom and speech, and the rejection of the sacraments.[10]

The Inquisition sought to inspire terror in those who came before it. The process of acquiring evidence started with an interrogation: a question-and-answer session taken under oath and recorded by notaries. Guilt was presumed from the start but if no confessions could be obtained by this method then mental and physical torture followed. This saved time and trouble, and the expense of a long imprisonment, but the torture was supposed to be moderate and to avoid spilling blood. Confessions given under torture had to be repeated away from the torture chamber, and at least two hostile witnesses were needed to condemn the accused. (There was usually no problem in getting these.) The Inquisition could then inflict the following punishments: for minor heresy prayers, discipline, fasting or going on a pilgrimage; for more serious heresy public humiliation, imprisonment or scourging, and for those who were heretics beyond redemption burning at the stake.

The trial continues

Everything had not gone entirely Philip's way. Clement reserved judgement for himself on Jacques de Molay and the provincial masters. This may have been a way of delaying proceedings further so that he did not

have to make a decision about the Order in the near future. Three cardinals were sent to Paris to interrogate de Molay and the provincial masters
on the pope's behalf. These accused men had been in the Order for many
years, often the whole of their adult lives. They had risen through the
ranks with the agreement and trust of their fellows, and the pope thought
that surely they could save the Order and its members. Instead they
repeated their confessions. The Articles of Accusation could stand.

Further delays followed. Clement's commissioners did not exert
themselves and the inquiry was dormant between August and December
1308. In slowing down proceedings Clement removed some of the initi-
ative from Philip. But Philip was an astute politician and could see
through Clement's delaying tactics. He urged Clement to stop prevaricat-
ing as it encouraged the Templars to revoke their confessions and claim
they had been given under duress. If Clement did not act all might be lost.
Those who had confessed and did not retract were to be promised absolution and life. Those who revoked their confessions were to be placed
in solitary confinement, on bread and water, and if they still persisted in
denying their crimes were to be tortured, and refused the sacrament,
absolution and a Christian burial. To make this strategy work Philip
kept control of the Templars in his own gaols, and torture by royal guards
continued.

Nevertheless, the delays went on. In August 1309 papal letters were
sent out to dioceses telling the bishops that Templar witnesses were to be
examined at the monastery of St Genevieve in Paris in November 1309,
and they should assemble there to hear them. The day set for this, 12
November, came and went, but no Templars appeared. Ten days later
they were still in Philip's hands and had not been delivered to the papal
commissioners. Was Philip reluctant to let the Templars speak in public
in case they decided to retract their confessions?

The Order's defence

So far the Templars had not said one word in their own defence. Kept in
solitary confinement they had no means of coordinating a defence. Now
Jacques de Molay and Hugues de Pairaud asked to appear before the
papal commission and defend the Order from the accusations made
against it. On 22 November seven men who claimed to be ex-Templars

appeared and said they too wanted to defend the Order. They were promptly arrested. But their appearance may have shown Philip that he should parade his prize prisoners, the Grand Master and the provincial masters, and let them condemn their order out of their own mouths.[11] De Molay, Pairaud and a few others were brought before the papal commission. When asked if he wanted to defend the Order de Molay said he was not learned enough, but would hold himself to blame if he did not try. Yet, he pointed out, he was a penniless prisoner, and had no one to advise him. The commissioners reminded him that he was on trial for heresy and that advocates were not allowed in heresy trials. They pointed out that he had already confessed and that in defending the Order he put himself at risk. His confession was then read out loud, just in case he had forgotten it.[12]

As it was read out, de Molay had some kind of seizure. He made the sign of the cross again and again and shouted at the commissioners that those who had heard his confession were evildoers and would be punished in the same way that the Saracens and Tartars treated their prisoners, by beheading or by being split in two. In his confusion de Molay turned to Guillaume de Plaisans, one of his original persecutors, for help. This is an indication of the weak state of his mind at this time, worn down as he was by imprisonment and hardship, as well as the vicissitudes of old age. De Molay was removed screaming from the court.[13] De Molay was followed into the papal commission's presence by a stream of Templars released by Philip IV. They claimed they wanted to defend the Order, though Philip hoped that by their statements they would condemn it once and for all. Ralph de Gisy came first, followed by Ponsard de Gizy, who named those he thought had betrayed the Order, while Brother John de Sarancorut, a servant, Brother John Verjus and others stepped forward to deny the accusations and to claim that the confessions had been wrung from them by torture. Compelling as this was, a royal gaoler produced letters allegedly written by Ponsard de Gizy to the pope asking the pope to search out the Order's faults as it was corrupt.[14] He was taken back to prison, a discredited and condemned man.[15]

Jacques de Molay reappeared on Friday 28 November. He was in no better state than before, incoherent and frightened. He said that he was a poor unlettered knight who had not the means to defend the Order. Instead he asked the commissioners to intercede with the pope on his behalf as the Order honoured the Church. It celebrated divine service in its churches, distributed charity, and had shed its blood in the service of Christendom. He reminded the commissioners that the Templars rode in the vanguard into battle, that countless hundreds of them had died in the Holy Land, and that Grand Masters had gladly given up their lives for Christ.[16]

The commissioners replied that they were concerned with souls, not bodies. De Molay affirmed that he believed in God, the Trinity and the Catholic faith, and that when he died God would see that his soul was pure. At this point Guillaume de Nogaret, Philip IV's chief minister, intervened introducing another line of inquiry. It was all very well for De Molay to claim the Templars had shed their blood for Christendom, but he had heard that the Templars were traitors to Christian princes and paid homage to the infidel. He had heard that the many defeats the Templars suffered in the Holy Land were the result of their sins. De Molay vehemently denied this, but added in his defence that William de Beaujeu had been forced to enter into truces with the Saracens and sultans in order to retain a foothold in the Holy Land. He and other young knights had been against this, as they were eager to fight, but had seen the sense of Beaujeu's policy and accepted it.[17]

Following de Molay's lacklustre performance the commissioners adjourned proceedings until February 1310. Philip IV must have realized that he had little to fear from de Molay and the other Templar officers, and that his best policy would be to let the Templars condemn the Order out of their own mouths. It was clear that no coherent defence would be forthcoming; the Templars were a spent force. Fighters rather than lawyers, they lacked the intellectual capacity and political acumen to defend themselves against accusations such as heresy. Let them appear before the papal commission, reasoned Philip and their own defence would show them guilty and condemn them. In a change of policy Philip began to move Templars from provincial prisons to Paris so that the papal commissioners could hear them testify. The final act in the Templars' tragedy was growing closer.

Notes

1 G. Lizerand, *Le Dossier de l'affaire des Templiers*, Paris: Librairie Ancienne Honore Champion (1923), pp. 31–5.

2 Lizerand, pp. 35–7.

3 Lizerand, pp. 39–43.

4 J. Michelet, *Le Procès des Templiers*, vol. 1, Paris: Les Éditions du CTHS (1987), p. 218.

5 Michelet, p. 75; vol. 2, p. 293.

6 T. Rymer, *Foedera* (1974 facsimile reprint), vol. 1, parts III–IV, pp. 99–100 is the text of the bull sent to Edward II.

7 Lizerand, pp. 57–63.

8 Lizerand, pp. 111–25.

9 Michelet, 1, 90–6.

10 M. Lambert, *Medieval Heresy*, Oxford: Blackwell (2005, 3rd ed.) p. 8; H.C. Lea, *A History of the Inquisition on the Middle Ages*, London: Sampson Low (1888), vol. I, pp. 79–80.

11 Lea, vol. III, p. 290.

12 Lizerand, p. 147.

13 Michelet, vol. 1, pp. 32–5.

14 Michelet, vol. 1, pp. 35–42.

15 Lizerand, pp. 154–5.

16 Lizerand, pp. 163–7.

17 Lizerand, pp. 168–9.

CHAPTER 9

• • • • • • • • • • • • • • • •

The Knights Templar at the stake

By 28 March 1310, 546 Templars had been brought to Paris from provincial prisons, and assembled in the gardens of the Bishop of Paris's palace. The papal commissioners asked that between six and ten of the brothers represent the Order. But these Templars were in a quandary. In defending the Order they would disobey their Grand Master who had originally told them to confess and be absolved, and they were bound by their oath of loyalty to obey him.

On 31 March 1310 the commissioners' notaries visited the places where the Templars were lodged to see whether anyone was prepared to defend the Order. All the Templars they spoke to claimed that the Order was pure and holy. They asked for the resumption of the sacrament, and for an assurance that they would be buried in consecrated ground when they died. They asked for clothes to cover their nakedness and for legal experts to advise them on how to proceed.[1] A letter to the commission from eight Templars who were lodged at the Abbey of Tyron complained that they were kept fettered in prison, and often had to spend the night in cold ditches. Their allowance of 12 deniers a day was insufficient to keep them as they had to pay 3 denier a day for their beds, the hire of the kitchen and clothes, 2 solidi and 6 denier a week to the smith who removed and replaced their fetters when they came before the commission, 18 denier a fortnight for washing, wood and candles, and 4 denier a day for the ferry across the Seine to get them to the commissioners.[2] This gives some indication of the harsh conditions in which they were being kept.

On 7 April 1310 representatives of all the provincial Templars presented a paper to the papal commissioners stating that they could not appoint anyone to represent them without the Grand Master's permission, but instead offered themselves as defenders. This meant that they were without a legal attorney, and had to rely on their own wits. They claimed that the charges against them were horrible lies made by apostates who had left the Order and wished to do it wrong. The confessions from serving brothers had been obtained by torture so terrible that some brothers had died under it, and would be accounted martyrs by the Church. They asked for assurance that those whose confessions had been obtained by torture would not be burnt as heretics. The commissioners responded by pointing out that they were not responsible for the Templars' treatment in royal prisons and were only concerned with the here-and-now. The Grand Master, they said, had been offered the chance to defend the Order, and had not done so.[3]

This portrayed de Molay in a bad light. It must have seemed to the assembled Templars that he had abandoned the rank and file of the Order to their fate by refusing to defend them himself, and by not giving them permission to take legal advice. It also shows how seriously the Templars took their vows of obedience. Even when death stared them in the face, they were reluctant to disobey the Grand Master.

Hostile witnesses in France

Four Templars, Renaud de Provins, preceptor of Orleans, Pierre de Bologna, Geoffroi de Chamberment and Betrand de Sortiges, indicated they would try to defend the Order, and they were present when hostile witnesses against the Templars were sworn in. Of 24 witnesses sworn, 20 were apostate Templars. On 13 April 1310 Renaud de Provins and his brethren claimed that the apostate Templars had been given royal letters promising them liberty and a large pension if they would confirm that the Order was corrupt.[4] This had no effect on the commissioners and the evidence from the hostile witnesses went ahead.

The evidence from the four non-Templars was mostly hearsay, amounting only to what the witnesses had been told by others, and not actually seen with their own eyes. As the commissioners went through the Articles of Accusation one by one, the witnesses agreed with them, and in places embroidered them. Master Ralph de Praellis, an advocate from the Laon dioceses, explained that he had become friendly with Brother Gervaise de Beauvais, the preceptor of the Templars' house at Laon, and had been taken into his confidence. Gervaise had told him that there were rituals in the Order so secret that no one outside knew about them, but they were written in a secret book that the king of France would kill to see. But asked about the other articles, he said he only knew that the brothers who were disobedient were imprisoned.

Nicholas Simon Domizell of Sens diocese, a priest, testified that about 25 years ago Janot of the Temple, his uncle, an elderly Aragaonese, and Arnulph de Visinall, knight of the Order, had told him that there was a secret book, and that they had heard about this from brother Gervaise. When he had asked Gervaise about it, Gervaise had responded, 'Ha!Ha! You have heard too much, say nothing.'[5]

The four outside witnesses were followed by the apostate Templars. Brother John of St Benedict, the preceptor of the Templar house of Bochard, said he had been in the Order for 40 years or more. He agreed that at his reception at Rouen he had been asked to deny Christ and spit on the cross. He said that the master had the power to give absolution from sins, but he had not seen any idol.[6]

John Taylafer de Gene of Lyons diocese, an ex-Templar, came to court clean-shaven and wearing a grey gown. He said he had entered the Order 25 years ago, and had left it three years previously, having lived in the Templar house of Mormont. He said brother Stephen the chaplain had received him into the Order, in the presence of six or seven brothers, but he did not recollect who they were. He was taken through the Articles of Accusation, and agreed he had denied Christ and spat on the cross, but only after he had been threatened with violence. He had heard that other brothers had trampled on the cross at their receptions. Carnal kisses were exchanged at his reception. He believed that the master could absolve sins. Asked about the idol he replied that on the day of his reception a head had been placed on the chapel altar. Asked if it was made of gold, silver, or wood, he replied that he did not know as he had not been allowed to get close to it, but from what he could see it was red in colour and the size of a human head. All the brothers present had venerated it. He was given a cord that he believed had touched the idol to wear under his shirt. After condemning the Order he added that he believed that in the house where he lived, alms had been given regularly. He said he had left the Order because it was corrupt.[7]

John Taylafer was followed on to the witness stand on 15 April by John English de 'Hinquemeta' of the London diocese. John had also thrown off the Templar mantle and was dressed in grey and had shaved off his beard. He said he had been in the Order for about 36 years, and had been received at Rouen by brother Peter de Madit, knight, the master of Picardy. After the Templar mantle had been placed around his neck he had been taken behind the altar and told to deny Christ and spit on the cross. Reynold, the chaplain of Rouen, had given him a white cord to wear under his shirt. He knew there was a secret book, but its contents were known only to the knights of the Order, and he knew that secret meetings were held. He had heard that brothers were permitted to have carnal relationships with each other, and he knew the master could absolve sins, but he had not seen any idol or any head.[8] The damning evidence continued. In the face of this there was little the Templar defenders could do but listen.

Philip of France was determined that there would be no coherent defence. He sought advice from an anonymous jurist who was set four questions to answer. The jurist came to the conclusion that de Molay's confession must stand as truth, as it had been confirmed by other brothers. Any retraction de Molay had made was nullified by the evidence. The secrecy in which the receptions took place condemned the whole Order, and the Order should be tried as a whole, rather than as individual members. As it was clear that the Order was corrupt and guilty as charged, the Church must act to eliminate the evil it had done; and as the whole Order was corrupt, individuals within it were also guilty and corrupt. In fact there was no defence for the Order, and it had put the whole Church in peril.[9]

Philip was tired of the vacillation of the papal commissioners, and he had friends amongst the leading churchmen in France on whom he could bring pressure. The first hint of what was happening elsewhere came on 10 May when the Templars still trying to defend the Order were called to an emergency meeting with the papal commissioner, and told that the provincial commission under the archbishop of Sens was going to prosecute any Templar who dared to defend the Order, or had revoked his confession. The Templars appealed to the commissioners to stop this, but it was too late. The archbishop was a friend and confidant of Philip, and his brother was one of Philip's chief ministers. He took no notice of the papal commissioners and swiftly condemned the 54 Templars who had dared to defend the Order to death by burning.

On 12 May 1310 the 54 knights, sergeants and servants were loaded into carts, and taken outside Paris to the field of St Antoine. There were no stakes set up for them, no chance for them to say their prayers. The horses were taken out of the carts, and the carts were set alight. The 54 men died horrible and painful deaths on that field. Nor was this the end of the burnings. The archbishop burnt four more Templars at St Antoine, and had the bones of John de Tours, the Templar treasurer, exhumed and burnt. The burnings spread across France. At Senlis nine Knights Templar were burnt at the stake on the order of the Council of Rheims; three Templars were burnt at Pont de l'Aude, and an unknown number in Carcassonne.[10]

Who were the Templars who died in May 1310? We know only the names of a few. One who we know for certain died at this time was Brother Anric of England, knight. Another was Ralph de Freynoy, and Galter de Bullein of Amboise, knight, and Guy and Martin de Nice, all described as 'burnt in Paris.'[11]

The Templars appearing before the papal commissioners in Paris were now in fear of their lives. On 13 May Aimery de Villiers, pale and trembling, threw himself on his knees and stretched out his hands to the altar asking God for sudden death and perdition if he lied. His audience expected a further confession, but instead he declared that all the crimes that the Order was accused of were false, and he had only confessed under torture. Then realizing what he had done he asked that the commissioners forget that they had ever heard him say this, and save him from being burnt as well.[12]

Hysteria set in amongst the surviving Templars. They did not know which way to turn. Should they confess to crimes they had not committed and live, or remain true to their consciences and the Order's Rule and die a painful death? The disappearance of Pierre de Bologna, one of the knights who had offered to defend the Order, snatched away and never seen again, took the heart out of the remaining defenders. They appeared before the papal commission and said they no longer wished to offer any defence of the Knights Templar. Proceedings against the Order were then adjourned until November 1310.[13]

Philip IV's tactics had worked. By political manipulation and personal pressure he had increased the climate of fear amongst the Templars, and destroyed their hope and confidence that they would survive. By condoning the burning of Templars without allowing them to mount a proper defence he had shown his power. Furthermore, he had managed to get the burnings done through the offices of the Church, which had the responsibility for condemning heretics. Clement could not object.

The papal commissioners reconvened on 3 November 1310 at the chapel of St Eligius in St Genevieve's monastery. Between November 1310 and May 1311 the commissioners heard the evidence of nearly 200 witnesses, both Templars and outsiders. Only 14 Templars denied the accusations against the Order and claimed that it was innocent of all crimes; 190 others stuck to their confessions, or revoked the retractions they had made. No one came forward to defend them. Many witnesses, such as John de Thora, a member of the Order for 40 years had taken off their Templar mantles. De Thora admitted all the Articles of Accusations.[14] Knights, priests, sergeants and servants all came before the commissioners. Most were frightened men, anxious to save themselves. The honour of the Order was forgotten, and it was every man for himself in a scramble to save his own skin. Most agreed that at the reception they were told to deny Christ as a false prophet and spit on the cross, and that carnal kisses were exchanged. One Templar, Hugues de Narsac, accused Jacques de Molay outright of immorality, and claimed to have seen him have carnal relations with his valet. Some but not all attested to having seen the idol in a variety of different forms. They agreed it might have been in the form of a head, but some thought it was a man with a beard, others that it was a woman.

The French Templars had condemned themselves, and the Order. The problem remained of what to do about the Order as a whole. Its dissolution seemed the obvious step, and this was probably the outcome that Philip of France had been aiming for when he arrested the French Templars in 1307. In order to settle the matter Clement V organized a council which was to be held at Vienne in France, starting in October 1311. At this council the Templars would be the main point of discussion. Summons to attend the council where sent out to leading churchmen across Europe.[15]

Jacques de Molay and other leading Templar knights remained in prisons in France. They were elderly men, worn down by hardship and cruelty, and at this point did not know their fate; but they were not alone. In Britain and across Europe there were Templars in prison who were still to appear before papal commissioners and argue their case.

Notes

1 H.C. Lea, *A History of the Inquisition of the Middle Ages*, vol. III, London: Sampson Low (1888), pp. 291–2; J. Michelet, *Le Procès des Templiers*, vol. I, Paris: Les Editions du CTHS (1987), pp. 47–53.

2 Michelet, pp. 150–1.

3 Michelet, p. 152.

4 Michelet, p. 165.

5 Michelet, pp. 175–7.

6 Michelet, pp. 179–81.

7 Michelet, pp. 187–95.

8 Michelet, pp. 195–7.

9 G. Lizerand, *Le Dossier de l'affaire des Templiers*, Paris: Librairie Ancienne Honore Champion (1923), pp. 70–83.

10 Lea, pp. 293–5.

11 Michelet, pp. 363, 509, 535, 538.

12 Lea, p. 296.

13 Michelet, p. 285.

14 Michelet, pp. 290–1.

15 The texts of these invitations/summons can be found in the archbishops' and bishops' registers for the period.

CHAPTER 10

The Knights Templar
on trial in Britain

Templar property in Britain

The Knights Templar were well established in the British Isles. They had property of some description in most counties of England, and commanderies in Ireland, Scotland and Wales. The hub of their operations was the New Temple in London, and outside London Temple Dinsley in Hertfordshire was an important Templar site. The English Templars elected masters for Ireland and Scotland, whilst the Welsh houses were administered from England. The masters for England are given in Table 10.1. The Templars divided England into baileys, and within each bailey there was a central administrative location. These commanderies were usually fortified manor farms with a chapel where the brothers could worship.

The Templars founded two new towns in England: Baldock in Hertfordshire and Witham/Newlands in Essex. Close to Witham, Cressing Temple still boasts the impressive Templar barns. The Order had a considerable number of holdings in Lincolnshire, Oxfordshire and Yorkshire, and hospitals for infirm and elderly knights at Denny in Cambridgeshire and Eagle in Lincolnshire.[1]

The Knights Templar's foothold in Britain followed a meeting between Hugh de Payens, the founder of the Order, and Henry I, king of England, in 1128. The Anglo-Saxon Chronicle describes this meeting and states that Henry gave Hugh 'great treasures of gold and silver, and sent him thereafter to England where he was welcomed by all good men: He then travelled to Scotland and received more treasures . . .'[2]

TABLE 10.1 ◆ *Masters of the Knights Templar in England*

	Master	Monarch
1140	Hugh de Argentine	Stephen
1150	Osto	
1154–64	Richard de Hastings	Henry II
1180–5	Geoffrey Fitz-Stephen	
1190s	William of Newburgh	Richard I
1200–18	Aymer St Mawr	John
1218–28	Alan Martel	Henry III
1229–48	Robert de Sandford	
1259–60	Amadeus de Morstelle	
1264	Ambersard	
1273–74	Guy de Forester	Edward I
1276–90	Robert de Turville	
1291–5	Guy de Forester	
1296–8	Brian de Jay	
1298–1313	William de la More	EdwardI/Edward II

Kings and queens gave generously to the Order in Britain. King Stephen and his queen gave them Witham and Cressing in Essex. Not to be outdone, Stephen's rival for the throne, the Empress Matilda, gave them an estate at Cowley in Oxfordshire, and her son Henry II added numerous parcels of land to the Templars' holdings. Subsequent monarchs added to these and confirmed the Templars' rights and liberties. Senior churchmen and noblemen and women followed suit and donated land, rents and other property. These donations were not solely a desire to keep in with and imitate the monarch, but had a deeper spiritual meaning. A donation to a religious order such as the Knights Templar ensured that priests would pray for the soul of the giver, his family and his ancestors, and thus shorten their time in Purgatory.

In Britain the Templars were very much part of the local community, and although there were quarrels with their neighbours which came before the courts, on the whole they were accepted, and they acted as any other lord of the manor would have done. They collected rent in kind (usually hens or eggs) or cash, and exacted labour service from their tenants. They held manor courts to sort out local differences, and attended the hundred courts where groups of manors met, and they sent their produce to local markets, and purchased commodities there such as herrings, staple food for Fridays among religious orders.

Apart from the New Temple in London, which was set within a large precinct, the lifestyle in the Templars' rural houses was simple. Each Templar had a bed, a tunic and a clothes bag. Meals were taken together in the hall and they worshipped together in a simple chapel. Some brothers helped to manage the farm and the tenants, but inside their precinct they led a monastic life of silence devoted to the worship of God. Like other monasteries their accommodation was shared with corrodians or pensioners who in return for a donation to the Order were given board and lodgings for themselves and a servant, and an allowance for new clothes.

The Knights Templar and the English Crown

The Templars in Britain were not only monks and farmers they were also part of the establishment. The Plantagenet kings relied on their counsel, and they embroiled the Templars in national and dynastic events. The generosity of King Stephen and the Empress Matilda was not entirely altruistic as they were engaged in a bloody civil war, in which both wanted the Templars' support, but apart from one incident the Templars managed to stay aloof from the conflict.

The Empress's son Henry II, who eventually inherited the throne, was quick to favour the Templars. He had vast lands in south-west France as well as the crown of England, and the network of Templar houses in both countries helped him to govern these. Richard I, his son, also favoured the Templars and many of the Order from both France and England accompanied him on the Second Crusade. When Richard left the Holy Land in 1192 it was in the guise of a Templar. Richard's brother John's policies had resulted in the country being excommunicated and it was the Templars who negotiated with papal envoys to get this reversed; it was also the Templars who lent John the nine golden marks which paid for his absolution. Brother Thomas of the Templars was in charge of outfitting the royal fleet for John and in 1226 he organized a muster of 200 ships for him.[3]

It was in the reign of John's son Henry III that the New Temple became an important administrative centre. The royal treasury was deposited there, and the master of the Knights Templar in England was given charge of the Great Seal when the vice-chancellor was out of the country. In 1229 Brother Geoffrey of the New Temple was appointed the king's almoner and Keeper of the King's Wardrobe. In this role he received and disbursed money for the king, purchased materials, and was responsible for the transportation of the state robes, and for equipping military expeditions. Large sums of money passed through his hands, as he was also responsible for collecting the Jewish tax. He was eventually dismissed from this office for refusing to sign a writ giving the queen's uncle, the count of Flanders, a toll of 4d on every sack of English wool exported to Flanders. There was no personal animosity between the king and Geoffrey, however, and Henry continued to send him gifts of wine after he was dismissed.[4]

Nobles such as Hubert de Burgh deposited their valuables in the New Temple, and like the French Templars the English branch of the Order acted as bankers for monarchs and their court. The New Temple became a place where the exchequer lodged its revenues. Henry III had what amounted to a current account with the Templars, and borrowed money from them using royal manors as security. The Templars also ran a messenger service taking money abroad for the king and his nobles. During the course of the thirteenth century over a million marks passed through the New Temple in London.[5]

Edward I, Henry III's son, held the Templars in high esteem. He had been on crusade himself and understood warfare in the East, and the resources it needed. The Templars were among his trusted councillors. The trust he put in them and the services they rendered for him are shown in a letter of 1304 to Jacques de Molay, Grand Master of the Knights Templar, when William de la More the master of the English Templars travelled to see him in Cyprus. Edward wrote asking de Molay to use de la More courteously and recommending his virtue. He asked de Molay to send him back to England speedily to govern the possessions of the Knights Templar in England for his (Edward's) honour. 'The king knows, and is grateful for the laudable services he has rendered to the king and his realm in many diverse ways, and the great affection that him and the brethren under him have for the king.'[6]

Edward I died in July 1307 and was succeeded by his son, another Edward. One of the new king's first acts was to seize £50,000's worth of gold, silver and jewels deposited by his father in the New Temple, and to give these to his favourite Piers Gaveston.[7] At the same time, Edward confirmed the Order's rights and privileges as his ancestors had done before him. Thus relationships between the Crown and the Order in England were generally amicable, and both parties looked forward to a long and mutually prosperous period during Edward II's reign.

The arrests of the Knights Templar in Britain

The arrests of the Knights Templar in France came as a shock and a surprise both to the English Templars and to King Edward. At first Edward refused to believe the accusations against the Templars, and wrote to the Kings of Aragon, Castile and Portugal suggesting they reject the charges and take no action. He also wrote to Pope Clement expressing his doubts about the guilt of the Templars, and his disgust at their arrest.[8] Had these kings acted together against Philip IV's high-handed actions the Templars might have been saved, but they did not and as we have seen Philip had an extra weapon in his armoury, his control of pope Clement who threatened excommunication to those who did not obey him.

On 15 December 1307 Edward issued secret orders to the county sheriffs telling them to choose 24 men of their county and 'summon them to the chief town of the county on the Sunday on the morrow of Epiphany (that is 5 January 1308) in the early morning, and there to execute the things contained in a writ to be issued to them by the king for the preservation of the peace.'

The next writ was issued on 20 December and was delivered by the king's messengers. It told the sheriffs to swear an oath before the messenger that they would not reveal the contents of the writ until it was put into action. They were to open the writ in the presence of the messenger and the 24 chosen men and read out the contents. These said that on Wednesday next after the Feast of the Epiphany they were to arrest the brethren of the Order of the Temple in their bailiwick and to make an inventory of all their goods and muniments. The Templars arrested were to be safely guarded away from their own places, but they were not to be placed in a 'vile and hard prison', and they were to be given sustenance.[9]

The secrecy of these instructions suggests that Philip IV had told Edward how to proceed, but the stipulation that after the arrests the Templars were not to be kept in hard confinement suggests that Edward was also exercising his own discretion. Sustenance for the Templars was to be paid for at a rate of 4d a day from their own estates, whilst William de la More, the master of the Knights Templar in England, who was arrested in Dover and taken to Canterbury Castle, received 2s 6d a day for maintenance.[10] At this time Edward was in a delicate position as he was betrothed to Philip's daughter and a marriage alliance between England and France was intended to stop the continuing warfare between the two nations. He did not want to do anything to jeopardize this match.

On 26 December 1307 Edward wrote to the Pope to tell him what he had done.[11] On a cold January dawn the Knights Templar in Britain were arrested, and taken to the nearest royal castle. Castles at Cambridge, Canterbury, Hertford, Lincoln, Newcastle upon Tyne, Oxford, Warwick and York became their prisons. In all 153 Templars were arrested in England and Wales, two in Scotland and 15 in Ireland. Only 15 of those arrested were knights, the rest were sergeants, servants and chaplains. Many were elderly and confused men, who did not come to trial but died in prison. The largest number arrested in any one place was at Denny in Cambridgeshire. Here 15 Templars were taken. Three died in prison and one, John de Hautville, was declared insane. Four of them had been in the Order less than ten years, the rest had an average length of service of 31 years.[12] Edward sent commissioners to run the Templar estates, with orders to send the revenue accounts to him.

At some point Edward's propaganda machine must have made efforts to exonerate him from blame for the arrests. The *Annales of St Paul's* states for 1308 that all the Templars were arrested by order of the pope.[13] Archbishop Greenfield of York seemed equally unwilling to act against the Templars. He made excuses that he had diocesan matters to attend to before he could be present at the trial, and in January 1309 he promised he would be in London to meet the papal commissioners, but then excused himself. His bishops were equally reluctant to act, as can be seen in the slightly desperate letters he sent to them, saying he could not possibly act alone in this matter, and promising them that the task would be as little irksome as possible.[14]

Compared to the French Templars the British Templars were lucky. They were not tortured by the king's gaolers, and they appear to have been in some kind of open imprisonment, allowed to go out into the town, and able to take their own goods in prison with them. However, they must have viewed the proceedings in France with foreboding. Edward married Isabelle of France in February 1308, and once that was done he turned his attention to his other concerns, namely protecting Piers Gaveston from the barons who hated him, and the Scottish wars. But he too must have watched events unfold across the Channel with misgiving and realized that it was only a matter of time before the papal inquisition arrived in England. He would then have some difficult choices to make.

Indications that the papal commissioners were on their way came in August 1308 when the archbishop of Canterbury and other senior churchmen received a mandate from Clement regarding the procedure against the Knights Templar. Their brief was to inquire into the affairs of the Templars in the provinces of Canterbury and York, Lund in Denmark, Armagh, Cashel, Dublin and Tuam in Ireland, Trondheim in Norway, and Scotland.[15]

Another year was to elapse before the arrival of the papal inquisition in the autumn of 1309. Hurried preparations had to be made then to trace the whereabouts of the Templars and to collect them into central places, as it seems that many had been allowed to return to their commanderies. Orders were sent out to the constables of the Tower of London, and Lincoln and York castles to expect to receive Templars from outlying locations. Similar mandates were sent to John Wogan, justiciary of Ireland, and John Seagrave the king's keeper in Scotland.[16]

These orders were not followed to with any great enthusiasm. On 14 December 1308 a further order had to be sent out to the sheriff of Kent to arrest all the Templars 'wandering about' in his bailiwick and to send them to London. Even when the Templars were received by the constables of the Tower and Lincoln and York castles they were not kept under control. On 12 March 1309 the sheriff of York was told to keep the Templars in his charge in such custody 'as he can answer for them at the king's order', as the king understood that they were allowed to move freely, in contempt of the king's order.[17]

The papal commissioners arrived in England to find a situation totally unlike that in France. There were no confessions waiting for them, and as English law did not permit the torture of freemen there was no easy way to obtain then.

The trial of the Templars in London took place between 20 October and 18 November 1309 in the Church of the Holy Trinity. The proceedings started with stating the names of those present, then the papal mandate was read out, and the 87 Articles of Accusation, based on the French confessions, were declared in Latin, English and French.[18] These were the same charges levelled against the Order during the French trial.[19]

The first witnesses to be heard were 47 Templars held in the Tower of London. They were asked how long they had been in the Order, who received them, where this happened and who was present. Some were asked what time of day the ceremony took place. This was variously stated as at midnight, between one and three in the morning or at dawn. They were then taken through the 87 Articles of Accusation based on the French confessions. All denied wrongdoing or said they did not know.[20]

Ralph de Barton, priest and keeper of the chapel at the New Temple, agreed that some brothers were received at a secret court, and he had heard they denied Christ and spat on the cross, but he had not seen this. He did not know about any idol, but agreed that at the reception all Templars were given a cord to wear under their shirts. Asked about the death of Walter Bachelor, a knight sent over from Ireland to be punished, he said he only knew he had been imprisoned in fetters, he did not know about his death. William de la Forde, who had been 40 years in the Order, said that they always observed the sacrament; and Thomas de Toulouse, knight, denied worshipping an idol as this was against the teaching of the blessed St Bernard.[21] Most said that they had taken vows of obedience, chastity and poverty at their reception and many of them had had to take an oath to aid the Holy Land. Robert de Sawtry, who had been in the Order for less than a year, was received at Balsall. He said the reception had been in secret and that he had had to swear that he would never tell outsiders what happened there.[22]

Three of those examined had been received into the Order abroad. John de Stoke, priest, had been received in Cyprus. He was also asked about Walter Bachelor. He said that Bachelor had received the sacrament before he died and had confessed to Richard de Grafton, a priest now in Cyprus. He believed Bachelor had been buried in consecrated ground by Ralph de Barton, now in the Tower.[23] Ralph, of course, had already denied knowing about Bachelor's burial.

Robert the Scot, arrested at Denny Abbey, had first entered the Order 26 years earlier at Castle Pelegrin in the East. He then left, but wishing to rejoin the Order had gone to Rome and received absolution from the pope and resumed the habit again at Nicosia in Cyprus. Himbert Blank had been at both his first and his second reception.[24] Blank, the preceptor of the Auvergne, was in England at the time of the arrests, and stood trial in London.

In December 1309 a number of witnesses hostile to the Templars were interrogated. Their evidence, at least in the eyes of the papal commission, was more fruitful. The le Dorturers, three public notaries, probably related to each other, gave evidence against the Templars. Robert le Dorturer said that he suspected the sometime master of England Guy le Forester of immorality as he had once enticed le Dorturer into a room and made advances to him. William le Dorturer testified that receptions and the chapter meetings were always held at night behind locked doors. Nicholas le Hurler said he had suspicions about the mode of the reception. John de Hodington, rector of St Mary, said he believed the Templars denied God. William de Beney, an Augustinian canon, reported a rumour that he had heard from a brother late of the Order at Duxworth to the effect that a brother of the Temple had said that no man had a soul, but was just like a dog.

William, the vicar of Sandwich, said that 15 years earlier a certain boy named John had heard that at Dinsley the Templars met in secret and worshipped a head. He had heard this was a very large head and he had hidden himself and had seen the brothers carrying it. Brother John de Gertia, a Minorite of London, said he had heard that 14 years earlier a woman called Cacoca, now dead, had hidden herself at the provincial chapter at Dinsley in a locked room, and had seen occult practices performed by the Templars. She had seen a black figure with shining eyes jump from a chest, and an idol on a cross, and had smelt a bad smell.[25]

Brother John de Donington, a Minorite of Salisbury, said the Templars had four idols at London, Bistlesham, Bruer and somewhere above the Humber. William de la More had, he said, 'introduced misery [sic] into England', and 'possessed a great roll with writings on it which were evil'. He said the Templars kept the idols in chests, and there came from the Holy Land and gave the Templars riches. He had been told all this by an elderly Templar called William de Sholerwick. William had also told him that he was in the Templars' hall when another elderly Templar named Daly came in and sported with him, and eventually they coupled, but this was not a sin, as there was a writ forgiving them. William Long had told the witness that there was a Templar who had left the Order and gone to the sultan and become his seneschal.[26]

In February 1310 some of the Templars who had already given evidence were recalled and asked about 24 'new articles' which included specific questions about denying Christ, spitting on the cross, sodomy and idolatry. Again the Templars denied the charges, but they admitted Templars were absolved by someone who was not an ordained priest. This may have been a misunderstanding of the word 'absolution' and what it meant as put to them by the inquisitors, as the master could absolve Templars who had erred against the Order in a chapter meeting.

The trial in London dragged on without result until March 1310 with the inquisitors putting increasing pressure on Edward II to allow them to get confessions by torture. The papal commission appealed to the bishops to help them persuade Edward, since Edward refused to see them and sent his answer to their requests by the bishop of Worcester, saying that he could do nothing without the consent of his earls and barons. He then left London, authorizing his council to give an answer – which they refused to do.[27] Edward seems to have given up resistance in early May 1310 when he sent orders to the sheriffs of York and Lincoln to do as they were asked to the Templars and their bodies, according to ecclesiastical law.[28]

A similar order did not go to the constable of the Tower of London until August 1310, when he was told to deliver the Templars imprisoned in the Tower to the sheriff of London when requested by the Inquisition. At the same time the sheriff was told to receive and guard the Templars and permit the inquisitors to do 'what they will with the bodies of the said Templars according to ecclesiastical law'.[29] It seems that John de Crumbwell, the constable of the Tower, was slow in complying with this as another order had to go out in October 1310. This time he was told that the Templars were to be lodged in solitary confinement in the four London gates, in the house of the late John Bakewell, and the houses of the penitent friars. They were to be well guarded and the inquisitors were to be allowed to do what they desired to the Templars, bodies, in accordance with ecclesiastical law. In effect Edward was passing the responsibility of the Templars in London to a civil authority, the sheriff of London, and more or less abandoning them to their fate.

The Templars in London were joined in March 1311 by those from Lincoln who had already been interrogated. Most denied all the accusations, but Robert Hamilton, who had been received into the Order 20 years earlier by Robert de Turville at Dinsley, said he had been given a cord to wear which he believed had touched a column in Nazareth. On his second examination he asked for forgiveness for his sins of the flesh. Henry de la Wold said he thought that the master could give absolution, but that was all.

The Templars examined in York were equally determined not to condemn themselves or the Order, but the hostile witnesses interrogated at York had some colourful tales to tell, all of which were hearsay or plainly made up to please the papal commissioners. John de Nassington said that Lord Milo de Stapleton and Adam de Everingham, secular knights, had been to a great feast at Temple Hirst where they saw the Templars worship a calf. Lord John de Eure told how, when William de la Fen of the Order of the Temple, preceptor of Wasdale, dined with him, after dinner he had given Eure's wife a book in which there was a slip containing heretical writing that Christ was not the son of God nor born of a virgin, but was the son of Mary and Joseph, and was a false prophet. De la Fen was questioned about this. He remembered the book but denied the heretical writing, and pointed out that Eure had waited six years to make the accusation. The Rector of Crofton testified that William de Reynbarr, an Augustinian canon now dead, had told him that Patrick de Ripon, a Templar now dead, had said that when he was received into the Order he had been told to deny God and Christ and to spit on the cross. Robert de Oteringham of the Minorites said that when staying at the Templars' house of Ribston, he had spied late at night upon the Templars worshipping an idol on an altar which faced west. The next morning when he asked about it he was told to say nothing about what he had seen.[30]

The inquisitors still lacked hard evidence and confessions which would condemn the English Templars. Eventually it seems that torture was applied, and it was used on Templars who had escaped and been retaken, namely Stephen Staplebridge and Thomas Tocci. It is interesting that Archbishop Greenfield had a longer list of apostate Templars which meant that some were still at large. The archbishop's list included Stephen Staplebridge but not Thomas Tocci, and also five others who do not appear to have been arrested: Ralph Buleford, Richard Engaine, William de Grafton junior, John de Pointon, and Walter Revel.[31]

Stephen Staplebridge confessed on 23 June 1311. He admitted he was an apostate and fugitive from the Order and accepted that he had been excommunicated in all the province of Canterbury and the town of Salisbury. His first reception had been according to the Rule. The second was two years later at Dinsley, where he was received by Brian de Jay the then master of England in the chapel. Present were Thomas de Toulouse, Richard de Herdwick, Roger de Reyley now dead, Ralph de Malton called the carpenter and Thomas Tocci of Thoroldesby. And with these present Brian de Jay collected a cross, and Roger de Reyley and Thomas Tocci drew their swords, and with Stephen between them together they said to the master, 'Do you see us, Lord?' and the master said 'Deny Jesus Christ is God and Mary was his mother and spit on the cross.' Stephen explained that he had been afraid for his life and denied Christ and spat on the cross. He said that all Templars had two receptions, the first a good legal reception, and the second against the faith. He further asserted that English Templars did not worship an idol or a cat, but he had heard that Templars overseas worshipped both. He also said that de Jay had told him that he must not believe in the sacrament, and that he believed the Grand Master could give absolution from sins. He was told that sexual relationships between other members of the Order were permitted and did not count as sin, and although he himself had not indulged, he had heard that Robert Hamilton had sexual relationships with an English juvenile. Asked about the death of Walter Bachelor, he said that he had died in prison by torture and he believed without cause. At the end of his confession he knelt and asked for mercy and forgiveness.[32]

In this confession Staplebridge had condemned not only the whole Order in Britain but individual members in it to possible death by burning. Thomas de Toulouse, Richard Herdwick, Ralph de Malton and Robert Hamilton had all denied the accusations against the Order under oath. Now they were in danger.

The second apostate was Thomas Tocci. He had been arrested and imprisoned in Lincoln Castle, but had bribed a gaoler to let him escape. He had fled to France and had heard many of the Templar confessions. He had then decided to return to England and give himself up to the mercy of the Church. He testified that he had been received into the Order 16 years earlier at Keele in Staffordshire by Guy le Forester. Present at his reception were Adam de Champmerle, Henry de Daumaris, John de Revives and William de la Beche Chaplain. Adam and Henry had drawn their swords and he had been forced to deny Christ and spit on the cross. He said the receptions were always held in secret. He described Brian de Jay's uncharitable attitude to the poor, throwing money into the mud so that he could see them grovel for it. He said that in the East the Saracens allowed the Templars to go in peace because they were allies. He too named brothers who had already denied the charges as being present at his reception. They included William de la More, Thomas de Toulouse, and Himbert Blank.[33]

The only part of this testimony for which there seems to be any evidence is that concerning Brian de Jay. There are other attested examples of his uncharitable acts and violence towards lay persons. When master of the Scottish Templars he had robbed a widow of her farm, evicting her by cutting off her fingers which were clinging to her door frame, and later murdering her son.[34]

The third Templar whose evidence condemned the Order in England was John de Stoke, a chaplain. Obviously he had been seen by the inquisitors as someone who would cave in under torture or even the threat of torture. Even though he had denied the charges under oath he now confessed to two receptions, one at Balsall 18 years earlier by Guy de Forester, and the second a year and 15 days later at Garway by Jacques de Molay. The second reception was in secret in a locked room. After he had promised the vows of chastity, poverty and obedience the master had asked him to look at a cross on which there was an image of Christ and asked him who it was. He said that it was Christ who came to redeem mankind. The master replied 'Wrongly said, this is the son of a woman, and it is said he is the son of God' and he was asked to deny Christ, which he did because two of the Templars had drawn their swords.[35]

Between them these three Templars had brought condemnation on the English Templars. As an example to the rest they made public confessions, were absolved and received back into the church, and sent away to do their penances. By this time the Templars in prison were probably aware of the burnings in France, and now Staplebridge and his colleagues had made it possible that the remaining brothers in England who had not confessed would meet the same fate. Fifty-seven of them came forward in London to abjure their heresies and be reconciled with the Church. Only William de la More and Himbert Blank resisted and would not confess, and were sent to the Tower of London. We will return to them later.

The Templars on trial in Ireland

The Templars were established in Ireland by 1177 when they were given the vills of Clontarf and Crook by Henry II. Members of the Anglo-Norman aristocracy followed his example, and the Templars acquired a considerable amount of property in Ireland, mostly on the eastern seaboard. They had preceptories in Carlow, County Dublin, Lough, Sligo, Waterford and Wexford; the whole adding up to valuable holdings worth at least £400 a year by 1308, producing a surplus of corn for export. They also bred horses.[36]

Although the papal commissioners were in Ireland by September 1309 the trial of the Irish Templars did not start until January 1310. However, preliminary enquiries had revealed that one Irish Templar, Henry Tanet, would be useful at the English trial, as he claimed that he knew the Templars made treaties with the Saracens – which had indeed been part of William de Beaujeu's policy when he was Grand Master. Tanet was duly sent to London. He seems to have come from a Templar family, since a Thomas de Tanet was mentioned by Richard Bistlesham as being present when he was received into the Order by Brian de Jay. Table 10.1 gives some details of the Templars brought to trial in Ireland.

Like their English counterparts the Irish Templars denied the accusations. Most of them had originated from England, and had been received into the order there, and many of them had English place-names as their surnames.[37] The usual crop of hostile witnesses appeared giving hearsay evidence and what they believed but had not seen. Brother Thomas, abbot of St Thomas Martyr by Dublin, denied making his evidence up, and swore on oath that he knew about the Templars' errors before the papal bull outlining these was published, and he believed that the Templars were culpable. Brother William de Botiller said he had been at mass in Clontarf and he saw that when the host was raised the Templars did not look at it. Other witnesses came forward with similar evidence.[38]

TABLE 10.1 ◆ *Irish Templars on trial*

Name	Years of Service	Place/person mentioned in connection with reception
Richard de Bistlesham	24	Brian de Jay
Henry de Haskelaby	20	Aslackby, Lincs.
Henry Tanet	7	Bruer, Lincs.
Henry Montravers	30	*unknown*
John Romayne	32	Willoughton, Lincs.
Hugh de Broughton	27	Bruer, Lincs.
Ralph de Bradley	5	Lidley, Wilts.
Adam de Langport	40	*unknown*
Richard de Upleden	30	Upleden, Hereford
Walter de Choreby	11	Ribston, Yorks
John de Faversham	23	London
William de Kilross	24	*unknown*

Source: D. Wilkins, *Concilia Magnae Britannae et Hibernae*, vol. II.

What they said did not really matter, as the fate of the Irish Templars was bound up with that of the English, and whatever happened to them would happen to those in Ireland. All they could do was wait the outcome of the English trial.

Templars on trial in Scotland

Only two Templars were arrested in Scotland, Walter Clifton and William Middleton, representing the two Scottish commanderies of Balantrodoch, now known as Temple in Midlothian, and Maryculter on lower Deeside. The Templars had other parcels of land in Scotland, a salt works in Callander and a tenement in Glasgow. They also had at least one tenement in each of the royal burghs, given to them by Alexander II of Scotland. But they were not autonomous like the Irish houses, as the English Templars oversaw Scottish affairs from the English general chapter.[39]

The two Scottish Templars were tried in the Abbey of St Cross in Edinburgh by the bishop of St Andrews and John de Solario, one of the papal commissioners during the winter of 1309/10. Walter Clifton said he was English and had been in the Order for ten years, having been received at Bruer by William de la More. Present at his reception had been Thomas de Toulouse, William de la Forde, Ralph the prior of the London Temple and many others. The Order's Rule was explained to him, and he swore on oath that he was not sick or married, and that he was free from debt. Then the master and the brothers present accepted him into the Order in the following mode. He knelt and joined his hands in prayer and promised service to the Order, the master and the brothers forever. The chaplain then held up a New Testament, on which a cross had been placed, and Walter took the book and the cross into his hands and took the vows of chastity, poverty and obedience by God and the Blessed Mary. Then the master gave him the mantle and put it over his head, and kissed him on the mouth. He then had to sit on the ground and unfasten his shirt, and was given a cord to wear under his shirt to remind him not to go with women. Asked if he had seen an idol, he said no and he did not believe in it.

He had been in Scotland for three years, and before that in London, Newsham, Rockley and Aslackby. He denied that the Order was corrupt, but he had seen the master make the sign of the cross when he absolved brothers in the general chapter.[40] Clifton's more detailed description of the reception has a certain ring of truth about it, as if he is describing exactly what happened, and it is closer to the reception of the Rule.

William Middleton had been in the Order for seven years, and had spent five years in Scotland. He explained how the Scottish Templars were administered and to whom they were responsible. He denied most of the charges, but said he had seen and heard the master of the Templars in England absolve brothers with the words 'By the authority of God and the Blessed Peter and the Lord Pope we commend, absolve you of your sin.'[41]

The hostile witnesses included the Abbot of Dunfermline who said that he had heard the brothers were received into the Order in secret and held their chapters at night. The Abbots of Saint Crucis, Newbattle, Brother Andrew of Dounvaid and others agreed with this.

Lay witnesses included William de Preston, William and Lord Henry Sinclair, and Adam Halliburton, who said that the Templars always held their meetings in secret and did not give alms. John Thyng, who had been the Templars' servant for 17 years, said that the Templars believed they could absolve those who had been excommunicated and that they practised the occult in their chapter meetings.[42]

The two Scottish Templars were eventually to make public confessions, and were absolved and received back into the Church.

The evidence against the British Templars was negligible. Apart from three confessions probably obtained by torture there was a general denial of the accusations, until eventually they capitulated when that appeared to be the only way out. Their main errors of judgement had been their secrecy, receptions and chapter meetings behind closed doors at night that had aroused suspicions, and given rise to wild speculations as to what went on, exacerbated by knowledge of the confessions by the French Templars and the Articles of Accusation.

Elderly Templars were allowed to confess their errors inside the church of St Mary, Barking.[43] Their younger brethren did it on the steps of St Paul's Cathedral. There we will leave them for the time being, awaiting their final fate. In the next chapter we will return to the continent and look at what happened to Templars elsewhere than France.

Notes

1 For further information on the Knights Templar in Britain and a gazetteer of places to visit see E. Lord, *The Knights Templar in Britain*, London: Pearson Education (2004 paperback edition).

2 G. Garmonsway, (ed.) *The Anglo-Saxon Chronicle*, London: Dent (1986), p. 259.

3 Lord, pp. 156–7.

4 Lord, p. 214.

5 Lord, pp. 221–5.

6 *Calendar of Close Rolls, 1302–1307* London: HMSO (1908), p. 208.

7 Lord, p. 240.

8 T. Rymer, *Foedera*, The Hague: Gregg Press Ltd (1967 reprint), vol. 1, parts III and IV, pp. 99–101.

9 *Calendar of Close Rolls, 1307–1313* London: HMSO (1892), pp. 13–14.

10 Close Rolls 1307–1313, p. 90.

11 Close Rolls 1307–1313, p. 49.

12 Lord, p. 83.

13 W. Stubbs, (ed.) *Annales Londensis*, Rolls Series 72 (1882), p. 265.

14 *The Register of William Greenfield, Archbishop of York, 1306–1315* London: Surtees Society (1931), pp. 145, 97, 281, 294–9.

15 For a version of this mandate see C.M. Fraser, *Records of Antony Bek 1283–1311*, London: Surtees Society (1953), vol. IX, p. 1301.

16 Close Rolls 1307–1313, pp. 175–7, 179, 181.

17 Close Rolls 1307–1313, p. 206.

18 The proceedings of the trial of the Templars are contained in Bodleian MS Tho. Bodlei. Oxon F.5.2. A printed version of these proceedings was published in 1737.

19 D. Wilkins, *Concilia Magnae Britannae et Hibernae* (1737), London, vol. II, pp. 329–33.

20 Wilkins, pp. 334–46.

21 Wilkins, pp. 337, 340.

22 Wilkins, p. 343.

23 Wilkins, p. 346.

24 Wilkins, p. 345.

25 Wilkins, pp. 348–9, 362.

26 Wilkins, p. 363.

27 Fraser, pp. 158–9.

28 Close Rolls 1307–1313, p. 200.

29 Close Rolls 1307–1313, p. 279.

30 Wilkins, p. 358.

31 Greenfield, p. 286.

32 Wilkins, p. 383.

33 Wilkins, p. 385.

34 Lord, pp. 188–91.

35 Wilkins, p. 385.

36 Lord, pp. 179–84.

37 Wilkins, pp. 373–8.

38 Wilkins, pp. 378–80.

39 Lord, pp. 185–95.

40 Wilkins, pp. 380–1.

41 Wilkins, p. 381.

42 Wilkins. p. 383.

43 The church of St Mary, Barking is situated beside the Tower of London.

CHAPTER 11

More Templar trials

The bull sent to Edward II of England by Clement V was also sent to Cyprus, where the Knights Templar had set up their headquarters after being expelled from the Holy Land, and to Germany, Italy, Aragon, Castile and Portugal, telling the princes of these states to act. Some Templars from these areas had already been caught up in the arrests in France; two German Templars were arrested on their way home, and at least one English Templar was burnt at the stake.

The Templars' trial in Cyprus

It was to Cyprus that the Templars had fled after the Fall of Acre in 1291. Here Jacques de Molay held court, receiving provincial masters of the Order and papal envoys. Here he also meddled in Cypriot politics.

The Templars were one of the richest landholders on the island, with seven large estates.[1] They had commanderies and churches in ten settlements on the island, concentrated in the north around Nicosia and Famagusta on the coast, and at Limassol and Paphos in the south, together with castles at Akrotiri, Gastria, Kolossi and Yermansaya. (See Map 11.1 for the location of Templar sites in Cyprus.)

In all 66 Templars were arrested on the island. At their trial they were questioned on the same Articles of Accusation as elsewhere. They all rejected the charges of denying Christ and spitting on the cross, and receiving illicit kisses at their receptions into the Order. They agreed that they promised not to leave the Order without permission, but denied

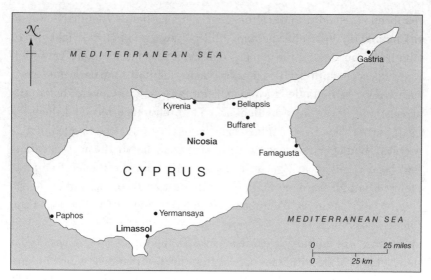

MAP 11.1 ◆ *Templar sites in Cyprus*

they were given permission to have carnal relationships with each other, and reiterated this when questioned about it for a second time. They denied any knowledge of an idol, but suggested, reasonably enough, that what some thought was an idol was in fact a reliquary containing a holy relic. All of them said that they had received a cord to wear under their shirts at all times, to remind them of their vows of chastity. They knew that if they revealed the Order's secrets to outsiders then they would be punished. They emphatically denied that they were not charitable. Every Templar examined on Cyprus agreed that each Templar house on the island gave one-tenth of all bread baked by them to the poor, as well as meat and other dishes, money and clothing. Charity was dispensed on three days each week, and even witnesses called against the Templars pointed out that the Order did not traditionally offer hospitality to travellers, but they would give lodgings to any good man, though not to women and children.[2]

The evidence from the Templars in Cyprus emphasizes the international nature of the Order. Many Templars there had been received into the Order elsewhere: received, in fact, by receptors whom other Templars had accused of corrupt practices. For example, Hugh of Mabii, knight, had been received into the Order four years earlier at Temple Newsham in England by William de la More. Philip Mews, an English knight also in Cyprus at the time of the arrests, had been present at Hugh's reception and had seen nothing illegal take place. Stephen of Valeria had been received by William de la More at Temple Dinsley, five years before the arrests, and Roger, another English knight, had been received there six years earlier. None of them had seen any errors. John 'the Englishman', a sergeant, had been received in Apulia ten years before the arrests. Others had been received in France by receptors whom the French Templars claimed had forced them to deny Christ, spit on the cross and exchange illicit kisses.[3] But the Templars in Cyprus denied that they had been forced to do this.

Neither did the hostile evidence against the Templars in Cyprus condemn them. Most witnesses agreed that the Templars were devout, and believed in the sacrament. Lord James of Plany, who had been at the siege of Acre, said he had seen them shed blood for Christendom, and he knew they gave alms to the poor. Lord Percival of Mar, a Genoese citizen, had heard it said that 40 Templars had been captured at Tortosa ten years earlier, and had been offered death or conversion to Islam, and had chosen death. The only fault the hostile witnesses found with the Order was their wealth, the way in which they acquired this, and their excessive secretiveness.[4]

It appears that the further away from Philip IV and Clement V, the more likely the Templars were not to confess, and the more likely witnesses sworn against them were to give their own opinions, and not repeat hearsay evidence, or make up what they thought the papal commissioners wanted to hear. However, the hostile witnesses elsewhere tended to be members of other religious orders, where in Cyprus they were predominantly lay persons and often members of the nobility; and many of them had fought in the East beside the Templars.

Templars on trial in Eastern Europe, Germany and Italy

Germany and Eastern Europe were also far removed from Philip of France and Pope Clement, but in Germany the Teutonic knights were dominant, and there were fewer Knights Templar than elsewhere. However,

they were responsible for a nunnery at Muller and scattered small commanderies. In Eastern Europe the Templars had some land in Croatia,
Hungary, Slovenia and Poland, and a house in Prague.[5]

Templar trials in Germany took place at Magdeburg and Mainz, and
the archbishop of Magdeburg may have executed some Templars, but
three Templars were acquitted at Mainz.

Germany was at this time a loose confederation of princely states and
archbishoprics. Italy too was a collection of city-states, republics, small
kingdoms, and papal possessions. The Templars had commanderies in
Abruzzi, Ancona, Apulia, Lombardy, Sardinia, Sicily, Rome and Tuscany,
amounting to 30 houses in total. The Templar trials in Italy took place
between 1309 and 1311 in places including Bologna, Brindisi, Florence,
Ravenna and the Papal States.

The evidence at these trials suggests that many of the commanderies
were tiny; some even too small to have their own chapel. None of the
Italian Templars appear to have ever left Italy, and Gilmour-Bryson suggests that they came mainly from peasant stock.[6] They were charged with
the same offences as at other trials. Some admitted to the accusations,
probably because torture was applied, although that is not proven.
Egidius the preceptor of Florence admitted denying Christ as a false
prophet, and claimed that he had seen others trample or spit on the cross.
He believed that some brothers practised obscene acts, and that idols
were worshipped in some Templar houses. Another Templar witness
claimed that they worshipped a cat in Bologna.[7] In 1309 the Templars
imprisoned in the papal prison at Viterbo were given the chance to
defend the Order. They refused.[8] However, it must be remembered that
all Templars were still under a vow of obedience to the Grand Master,
and he had not given them permission to defend the Order, or to hire
attorneys to do this.

The Italian Templars showed the same confusion as the English
Templars when it came to a lay person giving absolution from sin. Like
the English they confused this with the absolution given at chapter meetings for errors against the Order. Some Templars in Italy thought that
there had been a papal dispensation giving permission to an unordained
member of the Order to absolve from sins.[9] Had this happened, and there
is no evidence that it did, it would have been a practical device for the
Templars and other military orders to use when they were on campaign.

One Italian Templar who had left the Order before the arrests, Andreas Armanni, a sergeant, had been married when he joined, but had been given permission by his wife to become a Templar. He had only remained in the Order for a year, before returning home to the marital bed. Armanni confirmed many of the accusations. At his reception he had denied Christ and spat on the cross. He had been told that Christ was a false prophet, and that he should not have any confidence in salvation. He claimed to have seen a three-headed idol, which he was told would bring great riches to the Templars, and was worshipped by them. Another Italian apostate said that he had been told that the idol was the head of a Saracen. Gerald de Placentia, a sergeant, who had been in the Order for 24 years, said that the idol had one face and was made of wood. Another claimed that it was made of metal. Vivolus de St Justine, another sergeant, who had been in the Order for nine years, said it was a white head with the face of a man.[10]

Most of the Italian Templars agreed that the Order conducted its affairs in secret. They agreed that they had denied Christ, spat on the cross, and received illicit kisses at their receptions. Some suggested that these practices had been introduced long after the Order was founded.[11]

The Italian Templars were excommunicated, but this was reversed by penance and absolution. Those who were interrogated were mostly unlettered men, whose function in the Order had been to run its farms and vineyards. Any heresy they committed was purely accidental and done through misunderstanding. But they had agreed to illegal practices at their reception, and this seems to have been universal. However, as one Italian Templar suggested, it could have been a practical joke on the initiate.[12]

Resistance in Aragon

There was some token resistance to the arrests in Germany, but as we have seen the Templars were not numerous there. In Iberia however the Templars were ensconced in castles and armed ready for war, since they were in the front line of protecting Christians in Iberia from the Muslim Moors. They were not going to be arrested without a struggle, and like Edward II, King James of Aragon did not believe in the Templars' guilt. He received news of the Templars' arrests from Philip IV on 16 October

1307. He then wrote to the kings of Castile and Portugal suggesting that they needed more information before they acted. The text of Jacques de Molay's confession was sent to him on 27 October which shook his confidence.[13] But he did nothing until he received the papal bull, and only then did he order the arrest of the Templars in his kingdom.

This was easier said than done. As we have seen, the Templars in Aragon were already occupying defensible castles, and many of James's subjects supported them. Towns close to the Templars' castle opposed their arrests, and before he could besiege Templar castles, James had first to pacify the towns. This took some time, and military action did not start against the Templars until early 1308.[14]

The Templar castles in Aragon were strongly defended, and many were built on rocky prominences jutting out into the sea. Sieges in medieval warfare were often prolonged affairs, and provided the defenders had enough food, water and arms they could hold out indefinitely, and rain down missiles on the hapless attackers as they struggled to build and operate siege machines. Furthermore, the attackers had to scour a countryside already denuded of supplies for provisions. The camps of both side became littered and unsanitary, and dysentery killed more people in siege warfare than did fighting. Once supplies had run out, some sort of compromise had to be made, and many sieges ended with a truce, rather than a breach in the walls.

The first castle to fall to James was Libroo, in April 1308. Miramet on its promontory overlooking the sea was more difficult to take, and as well as the Knights Templar defending it, it had been garrisoned with outsiders who thought that the Templars were innocent. James seems to have shown a reluctance to kill the Templars and take the castles by force. He wanted the Templars out of their strongholds, but dead knights and destroyed castles were no use to him in defending his frontiers. He offered safe conduct to the Templars if they surrendered. At first they refused but eventually Miramet surrendered in December 1308, though Monzor and Chalomera held out until May 1309.[15] James now had the Templars where Philip IV and Pope Clement wanted them, in prison awaiting trial.

The resistance in the Aragonese castles was the only real fight the Templars put up against their arrests. The French Templars were taken by surprise and had little chance to resist. The English Templars were

aware of what had happened in Fance, and could have armed themselves, but made no attempt to resist arrest. This may have been due to
the age of many of the English Templars, and also to their lack of experience of military service. The inventories taken of their possession when
they were arrested show that there were few arms stored in English commanderies, and those that were found were often old and broken. It is
possible that the knights and sergeants had swords with them, and all
medieval people carried knives, if only for cutting up their food. The
only mention of a Templar sword being used in anger in Britain at any
time was when Brian de Jay, as master of Scotland, had used his to evil
effect. But on the whole the Templars in England and France seem to
have been remarkably unwarlike. Similarly, in Cyprus, the only place
where Templar knights outnumbered the sergeants, there seems to have
been no resistance to arrest.[16]

The trial in Aragon

About 200 Templars were eventually arrested in Aragon, but only 71 of
them ever gave evidence.[17] The procedure at the Aragonese trial followed
that in other countries. The evidence was taken under oath, and the
Templars were asked about the length of time they had been in the Order,
where they had been received, by whom and who was present at the
time. Forey shows that the Templars arrested in Aragon had been in the
Order for considerably less time than elsewhere, and were on the whole
younger than elsewhere. As many as 68 per cent were under 29 years,
and 32 per cent had been in the Order for less than ten years.[18] This must
reflect the front-line defensive position of Aragon, where Templars were
likely to see active service.

Two of the Aragonese Templars had been received in the East, and the
rest in Aragon. All of them denied that anything untoward had taken
place at their reception. But like the English Templars they seemed to
have misunderstood the rule about absolution and thought that the master could absolve sins. Forey suggests that while under siege in their castles, they had time to harmonize their stories, as their testimonies were
similar.[19] However, they were under oath so it is possible that they told
the truth, plain and simple. Even the witnesses against the Templars in

Aragon had little to add. They agreed that the Templars were secretive. One suggested that they had a silver head, surely a reliquary, and another had seen a carved head on a wall,[20] a gargoyle to drain off surplus water, perhaps?

Peter Olivous gave evidence under oath that he had heard from Ferrar de Bilget, the king's confessor in Tarragona, about a head possessed by the Templars which Ferrar de Liteto had seen carried in a cloth, and when revealed was a silver head with a beard. Another witness said he had heard that the Templars had evil secrets.[21]

The unsatisfactory results of the trial in Aragon were sent to Clement in March 1311. He sent back instructions to James that torture was to be used to get confessions. James was now in a quandary. He had promised the Templars when they surrendered that they would not be tortured, but he capitulated and allowed eight Templar sergeants to be tortured. They persisted in their denials of the accusations.[22] Forey suggests that unlike the French Templars to whom torture came as a shock, the Aragonese Templars had had time to prepare themselves for the ordeal. But as they continued to deny the charges under duress, this may reinforce the view that they were telling the truth, and were determined to keep their oaths of loyalty to the Order and to God.

James's ambivalent attitude to the Templars and to the treatment commanded by the pope continued after the torturers had finished. Those who had been tortured were given special care, ordered by James but paid for out of Templar revenues. Whilst the Templars were in prison their iron shackles were removed. They were allowed to take their own bedding and clothes into prison, and could receive gifts of food and clothing; and their daily maintenance was set at a higher rate than that of their guards.[23]

No confessions were obtained in Aragon. The Templars in that kingdom awaited their fate in relative comfort, whilst Clement called the Council of Vienne to consider their fate.

Notes

1 P. Edbury, 'The Templars in Cyprus' in M. Barber (ed.), *The Military Orders. Fighting for the Faith and Caring for the Sick*, London: Variorum (1994), pp. 189–95.

2 A. Gilmour-Bryson, *The Trial of the Templars in Cyprus*, Leiden: Brill (1998), pp. 32–6.

3 Gilmour-Bryson, *Cyprus*, pp. 87–100, 175–200.

4 Gilmour-Bryson, *Cyprus*, pp. 53–75.

5 H. Nicholson, *The Knights Templar. A New History*, Gloucester: Sutton (2002), pp. 130–1.

6 Gilmour-Bryson (1982) *The Trial of the Templars in the Papal States and the Abruzzi*, Vatican City: Biblioteca Apostolica Vaticana, p. 47.

7 Gilmour-Bryson *Papal States*, pp. 23–5.

8 Gilmour-Bryson, *Papal States*, p. 33.

9 Gilmour-Bryson, *Papal States*, p. 37.

10 Gilmour-Bryson, *Papal States*, pp. 42, 44, 49–50.

11 Gilmour-Bryson, *Papal States*, pp. 46–7.

12 Gilmour-Bryson, *Papal States*, p. 48.

13 H. Finke, *Pappstum und Untergant des Templeorden*, Munster: Druck und Verlag der Aschendorffschen Buckhandlung (1907), pp. 46–7; A. Forey, *The Fall of the Templars in the Crown of Aragon*, Aldershot: Ashgate (2001), p. 4

14 Forey, p. 24.

15 Forey, pp. 26–8.

16 Gilmour-Bryson, *Cyprus*, p. 31.

17 Forey, p. 76.

18 Forey, p. 78.

19 Forey, p. 79–80.

20 Forey, p. 81.

21 Finke, pp. 373–5.

22 Forey, pp. 85–6.

23 Forey, pp. 97–9.

CHAPTER 12

The supression of the Order and the fate of Jacques de Molay

Over sixty Templars had been burnt at the stake in France, but Jacques de Molay and other high officers of the Order still languished in prison. De Molay was probably still convinced that Clement V had reserved his trial for himself, and he would be saved. He had confessed to the accusations, retracted his confession, and then denied the retraction. He had offered no defence of the Order, and had given his fellow Templars no permission to seek out legal aid to do this. In other words he had failed the Order and his brothers. But in 1311 at the Council of Vienne he still did not know his fate.

The Council of Vienne

Archbishops from every country in Europe were summoned to the Council of Vienne.[1] Many refused to go or found excuses to avoid the summons. They knew that the chief topic to be discussed was the guilt of the Templars, and what to do with the Order and its possessions, and they did not want to get involved.

The council opened on 16 October 1311, when Clement himself preached a sermon in Vienne Cathedral. In the sermon he asked the council to consider the verdicts from the trials and to decide what should happen to a religious order that according to the evidence was manifestly corrupt. But to be fair to Clement he had asked the Templars to send representatives to defend their Order to the council.

Seven Templars duly appeared, followed by two more. They claimed that there were 2,000 Templars at large and armed and hidden in the area around Lyons.[2] With hindsight this claim seems unlikely, but council members had no idea how many Templars had escaped arrest, or how many there had been in the first place. The council was thrown into panic, expecting the 2,000 knights to descend on them and murder them in their beds. The nine who had appeared were arrested, and the fabled 2,000 did not show up. This incident made some of the council members think more deeply about what they were doing. Some began to demand that the Templars be allowed to put their defence to the council, and it soon became clear that apart from the French prelates the rest had doubts about the evidence they had been given. An English monk present at the council suggested that the French only agreed with the evidence through fear of Philip IV.[3]

Philip meanwhile was waiting impatiently for news that the Knights Templar had been suppressed. When his agents reported back to him about the growing opposition to the suppression of the Order, doubts about the confessions, and a growing clamour to allow the Templars to defend themselves, he could see that Clement was losing control of the situation. The council dragged on into the spring of 1312 with Clement arguing for the suppression of the Order, but others saying that the Templars must be heard. The council was at a stalemate. It was time for Philip of France to act. He arrived in Vienne with an armed force, accompanied by his sons and the king of Navarre. The council now had to choose between the supposed secret army of Templars or the harsh reality of Philip's armed thugs. The feeling of the council changed. Now most delegates agreed that the Knights Templar must be suppressed.

On 22 March 1312 Clement drew up the bull *Vox in excelso* to abolish the Order of the Knights Templar. No doubt Philip was looking over his shoulder as he dictated it. On 3 April 1313 the bull was read out to the council. It condemned the Order because of the scandals surrounding it; its secret meetings and illicit receptions that were against the Christian faith and its detestable idolatry and its practice of sodomy. Clement reserved the right to dispose of the Order's possessions as he thought fit, and then drew a line under the whole affair declaring that any further discussion was pointless. The trial of the Knights Templar was over. They no longer existed.

Disposal of the Templars' property

There remained the question of what would happen to the Templars' possessions. No doubt Philip IV waited eagerly to receive his reward and an end to his financial problems. It was not only their revenues Philip wanted but the Templars' land as well. This would give him political control over swathes of land in south and south-western France, in Normandy and elsewhere, and make him of by far the greatest landowner in the country, which would diminish the power of the Church and other lords. Other Christian princes also waited to see what they might get. James II of Aragon and the other Iberian princes still had to protect their borders against the Moors. Edward II of England had found the revenues from the Templars' estates a useful addition to his income, and he had denuded the properties of timber and other resources, as well as giving Templar land to his supporters. In England families whose ancestors had granted the Templars land had taken this back when the Templars were arrested. In fact the whole of Europe wanted to know who would get the Templar estates.

Their answer came in the bull *Ad providem* which was made public on 2 May 1313. This stated that the Templars' property was to go to the Knights Hospitallers, except for that in Iberia, which Clement would deal with later. Had Clement at last stood up to Philip IV and thwarted his ambition to control the Templar estates in France? In order to circumvent any interference with the Knights Hospitaller taking over the Templar estates, Clement issued a mandate that anyone preventing the Hospitallers from entering into what was rightfully theirs would be excommunicated. Philip, who had started the persecution of the Templars, was left with nothing, and no chance of taking over the Templar estates by force. However, he could still bring pressure to bear on Clement by threatening to re-open the charges against Pope Boniface. Eventually Clement absolved Philip from all the debts that he owed to the Temple in Paris and gave him 200,000 *livres tournois* as compensation for alleged losses incurred by placing the royal treasury into the Templars' hands. This was to be paid in three instalments, but Philip was dead before the final instalment was made.[4]

The discussion on what was to happen to Templar property in Iberia continued. The Iberian princes wanted the property to pass into their hands rather than those of the Hospitallers, as the latter might over-stretch the Knights Hospitaller, who were thin on the ground in Iberia and compromise border defence. Nothing was resolved about Aragon until after Clement's death, when in 1317 Pope John XXII gave permission for James II to found a new order of knights, and to use the Templar property to fund this. The king of Portugal was also given permission to form a new order of knights using Templar revenues, which became the Order of Christ. In Castile the Hospitallers spent years trying to enter into possession of the Templar estates and collect the revenues.[5]

The Hospitallers also had serious problems in taking over the Templars' property in Germany. A group of renegade Templars reoccupied the fortress of Hildesheim and had to be evicted by force. In Italy too there were similar problems, as princes and city fathers were reluctant to hand over the Templar possessions. But in Cyprus the transfer went smoothly.[6]

In England things did not go at all smoothly for the Hospitallers. It took them until 1324 before they had access to the majority of the Templar properties. When they eventually entered these they found the estates and their buildings in disrepair, stripped of their resources and livestock and charged with heavy outgoings as the revenues were not only used for the Templars' maintenance but for their pensioners as well.

On receipt of the bull passing the Templars' property to the Hospitallers Edward II had done nothing, but as a delaying tactic had referred the matter to parliament, refusing to hand over the lands to the Grand Prior of the Hospitallers in England without parliament's permission.[7] Earlier inquiries by the papal commissioners about the Templar property in England should have alerted them to what might happen. In 1310 Anthony Bek, patriarch of Jerusalem and bishop of Durham, claimed that Edward, who was involved with various 'notorious difficulties', would not release any information about the Templars' property or give an audience to the papal commissioners.[8]

In 1338 the Hospitallers made an inventory of their lands. This included a list of the Templars' property that they should have received but had not, which amounted to 15 estates in total, worth 1,379 marks a year, a considerable sum of money.[9]

What happened to individual Templars

Although the Order had been suppressed its members were not released from their religious vows, in other words they were still monks if not knights. Provision had to be made for them in other religious houses where they could do penance and receive absolution. Until the amount they could receive was restricted by the pope, some received generous pensions, and some went back to live in their old preceptories.[10] Others released from the confines of the preceptory seem to have gone wild. In Aragon an ex-Templar named Berengar de Pulcrovisa took a concubine, and Martin de Frigola was accused of rape.[11] Some absconded from the monasteries where they had been sent and married. But they had nothing to lose. The discipline of the Order had gone, they had been discredited; they must have thought: why not live an ordinary life, hopefully in comfortable obscurity?

The English rank-and-file Templars were sent to monasteries with a pension of 4d a day. This was well above what the average daily rate that a labouring peasant could expect. The Templars were distributed to the dioceses of Bath and Wells, Chichester, Coventry and Lichfield, Ely, Hereford, Lincoln, London, St David's, Winchester and Worcester (see Box 12.1).

William de la More, master of the English Temple, steadfastly refused to accept the absolution, claiming he was innocent of all crimes. He was sent back to the Tower of London where he died in 1311 leaving goods worth £4 19s 11d.[12] Himbert Blank, the master of the Auvergne and the Templar Visitor also refused to admit to any of the accusations. On 6 April 1313 he was delivered to the archbishop of Canterbury and placed into his custody with maintenance of 2s a day.[13]

Not all of the English Templars placed in the care of monasteries settled down gracefully. In the archdiocese of York 15 Templars refused to remove their Templar mantles, and Thomas de Stanford, sent to Fountains Abbey, abused the community there, when they tried to make him take off his Templar robe.[14] There were soon complaints from the heads of the monasteries and abbeys where the Templars had been sent

Box 12.1 Where English Templars were sent after the Order was dissolved

Chichester diocese
Henry Paul
John Standon

Worcester diocese
John de Coningston
John de Balsall
John de Whaddon
William de Scotho
Henry de Wychale

Lincoln diocese
Simon Stretch
John Stoke
William de la Ford
William Raven
Thomas Chamberlain
Hugh de Tadcaster
William de Sautre
William Burton
Roger Norreys
Thomas de Ludham
William de Chelsey
Alan de Newsom
John de Sadlescombe
William de Bernewelle
William de Hedington
Peter de Otteringham
William de Pocklington
William Thorpe

St David's diocese
John de Wirekeley

Hereford diocese
Thomas de Whotop
Salisbury Diocese
John de Mohun
John de Eagle
Robert Hamilton
Robert de Sautre

Ely diocese
Robert Scot
Roger Dalton

Norwich diocese
Robert de Spanneta
John Coffyn
William de Wynton
William de Chesterton
Ralph Tanet

London diocese
Richard Peitevyn
William de Welles

York archdiocese
William de Groston
Ralph de Roston
Thomas de Stanford
Henry de Kerreby
Thomas de Bellerby
Robert de Langton

William de la Fenne
Richard de Keswick
Stephen de Radenach
Michael de Sowerby
Godfrey des Arches
John de Walpole
Ivo de Etta
Henry de Craven
Roger de Huginden
Henry de Romlif
Geoffrey de Witham
Walter de Gaddesby
Richard de Ripon
Thomas Stretch
Roger de Shelfold
John de Ebreston
Walter Middleton
William Clifton

that the maintenance payments they were expecting to receive out of the Templar estates were in arrears.

The English Templars had survived the trials and their punishment was relatively light. However, in France the Grand Master Jacques de Molay and his colleagues still awaited their fate.

The fate of Jacques de Molay

The Order was suppressed in 1312. Two years later Jacques de Molay, Geoffroi Charney the preceptor of Normandy, Hugues de Pairaud and Geoffroi de Gonneville were still in prison. They remained convinced that Clement would save them, as he had indicated that he and he alone would pass judgement on them. But Clement delayed taking any action until December 1313 when a commission was appointed to examine de Molay and his colleagues. Whether or not the decision to hold the inquiry in Paris was influenced by Philip IV is not clear, but the result was that the cardinals and the prisoners were under the king's control.

The four Templar prisoners came before the commission of cardinals on 18 March 1314. They were elderly men who had spent seven years in prison under harsh conditions. Jacques de Molay was confused and he must have been aware that he had betrayed the Order by his confession given so quickly under duress, and by failing to defend the Order adequately, or giving permission for others to do so.

De Molay and the others had already confessed to the accusations in full. Now perhaps knowing it was his last chance to redeem his conscience and clear the Order's name for posterity de Molay stood before the cardinals and once more retracted it. He denied everything he had confessed to, and told the cardinals that the Order was innocent of all accusations made against it. Geoffroi de Charney followed him, and also retracted his confession.

The cardinals were thrown into total confusion. Had they expected a meek admittance from de Molay that his confession was the truth? In that case he could have been absolved and sentenced to life imprisonment rather than death. In an act of cowardice the cardinals washed their hands of Templar business and handed de Molay and Charney to the civil authorities of Paris.

This was the moment Philip IV had been waiting for. He could now inflict his own punishment on men who had confessed to heretical and immoral practices. They should die the death of heretics and sodomites that very day. They were taken to a small island on the Seine and the stake was prepared. Now they seemed calm. The battle was over. Now they would share the fate of their comrades who had already died by fire. Whether de Molay uttered the curse put into his mouth by Geoffroi de Paris cannot be ascertained. Other contemporary witnesses to the burning claimed he died heroically and still denying that the Knights Templar were guilty of the accusations.

Even if de Molay did not utter the curse against Philip IV and Clement V who had condemned him, people soon believed he had. Clement died in agony on 20 April 1314 only a month after de Molay was burnt, and Philip IV followed him to the grave on 29 November the same year.

The memory of de Molay's death lived on in France. When Louis XVI was guillotined in 1793 a member of the crowd stepped forward, dipped a cloth in the royal blood and held it up proclaiming: 'Thus is the death of Jacques de Molay avenged.' And was it coincidence that the royal family were imprisoned before their executions in the Paris Temple?[15]

Notes

1 *Registrum Clementis Papae V*, Rome: Vatican (1887), vol. V, p. 397.

2 M. Barber, *The Trial of the Templars*, Cambridge: CUP (1974), p. 224.

3 Walter of Hemingburgh *Chronicon Domum Walteri de Hemingburgh*, ed. H.C. Hamilton, London: HMSO (1865), Rolls series 82, pp. 292–3.

4 E. Lord, *The Knights Templar in Britain*, London: Education Pearson (2004), p. 262.

5 Barber, pp. 235–6.

6 Barber, p. 238.

7 Lord, p. 262; *Calendar of Close Rolls* 1307–1313, London: HMSO (1892), p. 544.

8 C.M. Fraser, *Records of Anthony Bek, Bishop and Patriarch 1283–1311*, London: Surtees Society (1953), no. 162, p. 158.

9 Lord, p. 263.

10 Barber, pp. 238–9.

11 H. Finke, *Papsttum und Untergand des Templeorden* I, Munster: Druck und Verlag des Aschendorffschen Buchhandlung' (1907), p. 383.

12 Lord, p. 259.

13 Close Rolls 1307–1313, pp. 521, 533.

14 R. Hill, 'Fourpenny Retirement: The Yorkshire Templars in the Fourteenth Century' in W.J. Sheils and D. Wood (eds), *The Church and Wealth*, Studies in Church History 24, Oxford: Blackwell (1987), p. 127.

15 Thanks to Colin Haydon of University College, Winchester for raising this question.

CHAPTER 13

Were the Knights Templar guilty?

The question as to whether the Templars were guilty exercised their contemporaries and has been debated by historians through the ages. Were the confessions, albeit obtained under duress, true, or were the charges trumped up by Philip IV who wanted, for various reasons, to destroy the Order? Was it indeed corrupt, in decline and lacking in discipline? Or were the accusations false from the start?

First we shall consider what fourteenth-century commentators concluded about the Templars' guilt; second we shall look at the verdict of historians; and finally we shall examine the evidence as presented in the trials, taking each group of Articles of Accusation and drawing conclusions from the statements on these.

The verdict of the Templars' contemporaries

It has to be remembered that anyone speaking out against the verdict, especially in France, was endangering his or her own life. The fate of the Templars acted as a warning about the absolute power of the State and the Church, and reinforced the warning given by the massacre of heretics at Carcassonne that deviation from the Catholic religion would not be tolerated. Thus anyone questioning the fate of the Templars would be wise to be circumspect about such questions. Most of the Templars' contemporaries accepted the verdict without comment. It was recorded in the chronicles as a deed done and over with. But of course most chronicles were written by churchmen, and this might not be a representative sample of opinion. Of the views of the majority of the population who were not able to record their comments in writing we know nothing. However, Giovanni Boccaccio, who was an eyewitness at de Molay's death, wrote that the populace were amazed, and many of them believed that the Templars were innocent, but dared not say so.[1]

One contemporary who did speak out was Jacques de Therries, a professor of Theology at the University of Paris, who in *Contra Impugnatores Exemptionum* made his position on the Templars clear. The crimes confessed to were horrible, but he could not accept the Templars' guilt. They were honourable men, from good families, he averred. They had taken religious vows and they lived by rules drawn up by a saint and approved by a pope. He asked how, if the perversions described did exist, had they entered the Order? And why had some Templars retracted their confessions when they knew the result would be death by fire, and the fires of hell in after-life because they had received no absolution?

Another Frenchman, whose name is not known, wrote a letter that condemned the proceedings against the Templars and addressed the academics of the University of Paris. The writer described his horror when the accusations were made known by 'that Gascon' (Esquin de Floyran). He thought the trial was unjust and the treatment of the Templars cruel. He too mentioned the rulebook and the Templars' valour in the Holy Land. He lamented the fate of those Templars who had died under torture, and argued for a fair trial for the rest.[2] As the writer appears to have been party to the original accusations by de Floyran he must have been someone close to the royal court. So it is no wonder that he wanted to remain anonymous.

Another contemporary, the Mallorcan Ramon Lull, thought that the Holy Land would only be re-taken for Christendom if the Knights Templar and the Knights Hospitaller were united. Jacques de Molay had been vehemently against this, and this prejudiced Lull against the Templars. He was obviously convinced of the Templars' guilt and emphasized this in his writings.[3] Dante Aligheri, who was living in Florence under French domination, used the Templars as propaganda against the French, in the *Divine Comedy*, claiming that the Templars were innocent victims of the machinations of Philip IV,[4] an idea that would appear again in later centuries.

The verdict of historians

As time elapsed following the suppression of the Order so different aspects of the Articles of Accusation were seized upon. Henry Cornelius Agrippa used as his model the witchcraft trials in sixteenth-century Germany, identified similarities with the practices attributed to the Templars, and decided that the Templars were guilty of using malevolent magic. In *De occulta philosophia,* published in 1531, he fabricated a colourful account of Templar occult atrocities, which remained in the public mind through to the twentieth century.[5] The Templars were used as an example of the way minorities could be persecuted by the powerful by Jean Bodin in *The Six Books of the Commonwealth,* published in 1581. From these instances it is clear that the Knights Templar could be used (and are still being used) to prove almost anything. Protestant writers could give the trial as an example of innocent victims persecuted by the Roman Catholic Church, or use the evidence given in the confessions to show the inherent corruption of that same Church. Catholic writers could use the confessions of homosexual practice and absolution by lay persons to show the corruption and ungodliness of the heretic.

It was not until historians began to study the actual documents from the trial that a more rational approach was taken. Even so, at the start of the eighteenth century the Dupuy brothers used the French Templar trial process to demonstrate, to their own satisfaction, that the Knights Templar were corrupt and always had been. The Dupuys were writing on the eve of the Enlightenment and the development of a philosophy based on scientific experimentation and rational thought. This changed the way in which the past was examined. Historians sought to replace conjecture with truth, and with the wave of scientific investigation went an interest in deconstructing myths and explaining away the occult. Conversely the growth of freemasonry and its desire to legitimize itself by acquiring a past led to the Knights Templar became a vehicle for this effort, leading to more research into the Order.

In the eighteenth century more national records became available for research. Wilkins published his printed transcript of the Templar trial in England in 1737, based on a document in the Bodleian Library. In England the public records were removed from the Tower of London and made more accessible, and work was started on transcribing and printing manuscripts in the British Museum, which became part of the 'Rolls' series. The printed transcript of the French trial was published in 1841, and reprinted in the twentieth century.

In the early nineteenth century German authors took up the occult theme suggested by Agrippa. J. von Hammer-Purgstall claimed he had identified the whereabouts of 30 Templar idols, while J. Prutz claimed that the Templars were guilty of a heresy that had infiltrated the Order's high officers.[6]

In mid-nineteenth century England the guilt of the Templars was taken up by lawyers from the Middle and Inner Temple, who began to examine the evidence in the light of the legal proceedings. C.G. Addison published his history of the Knights Templar in 1840. He used primary sources extensively, but was accused by his critics of producing a biased account in favour of the Knights Templar. He claimed, however, that all the evidence he had seen led him to believe that the Templars were not guilty.[7] An academic lawyer, J.G. Morshead, writing as 'Justice Shallow', used the evidence published by the Dupuys, Michelet's printed version of the Templars trial in France and Von Hammer-Purgstall's ideas, to conclude that the Templars did indeed spit on the cross and deny Christ, and that they worshipped an idol and committed other heresies. He suggested that these practices were introduced by fanatics in France.[8] In a fuller printed version he did not exonerate the Templars but suggested that it was a combination of personalities that led to their downfall. He described de Molay as a 'the most tragical figure in history. No saint and no statesman, his innate conservatism and lack of foresight led to his special disgrace, a ludicrous death, and the downfall of the order'.[9]

Morshead was one of the first commentators to attempt to analyse the Templars evidence statistically. He discovered that of 30 Templars examined in Paris in 1307 all agreed they had denied Christ at their reception, and all except one had spat on the cross. Nineteen had received carnal kisses, and 20 said they had received permission for carnal acts with other Templars. Five of them mentioned the idol; however, when this group of Templars who had already confessed were re-examined in 1310, only one mentioned the idol.[10] Morshead also examined the confessions of 225 Templars from the French provincial trials. Again all agreed they had denied Christ and most had spat on the cross. Eight mentioned an idol and three, at Orleans, Poitiers, and Tours, said the Templars worshipped a cat.[11]

In his typewritten notes Morshead suggested a gulf between the Templar elites and the rank and file, and postulated that it was the elite that were corrupt. He suggested that not all the confessions obtained by torture were false, and demonstrated a uniform rite used at receptions. Morshead then put forward the idea that perhaps the Templars had incurred Philip IV's wrath by financing Pope Boniface against him.[12]

In the 1920s E. Martin agreed with Morshead that the Templars had been infiltrated by fanatics who had introduced occult practices into the Order, and the idea of occult practices has persisted. Martin suggested that the Templars worshipped the devil in the form of a cat, but also pointed out that contemporaries had condemned the Templars' greed, ambition and avarice.[13]

E. Peters argued that the case against the Templars developed in the light of the general awareness of sorcery and magic in the late thirteenth century, which made the Church vulnerable (not to mention threatening Philip personally), and the kingdom in general. The papacy under Pope Boniface had accused Philip of being a tyrant, charges he countered with accusations of heresy, blasphemy, sorcery and sodomy against Boniface, together with a claim that the Church that accused him was not the true Church. Peters suggests that in Philip's mind the Templars became a surrogate for the Church. Although historians have questioned whether the charges against the Templars were true, Philip believed they were, and the general public in France seem to have believed it as well.[14]

As the twentieth century progressed, more imaginative and fanciful ideas emerged about the Templars, which will be discussed later in this book. These ideas have to be set against the reasoning of historians such as Malcolm Barber. He wrote in *The New Knighthood*, the definitive work on the Knights Templar, that by the time of the trial the Templars were in decline and a corrupt order. He thought there was a lack of discipline, and that what happened at the reception was horseplay.[15] However, he also thought that the charges of heresy were non-proven and that Philip IV was the motivating force behind the trials and the suppression of the Order.[16] In a paper about the relationship between Philip IV and the Templars' downfall, Barber showed how Philip manipulated propaganda with regard to the charges against the Templars, playing on public fears about magic, heresy and homosexuality, and invoking folk myths about a ghostly head.[17]

Discussion has continued about the Templars' guilt as historians have concentrated on themes from the trial that relate to contemporary social concerns, such as homosexuality. Anne Gilmour-Bryson pursued this element using the French and Italian trial evidence. She pointed out that some historians are convinced that the Templars were guilty of sodomy, even if they were not guilty of illicit kisses at the reception, and that sodomy could have originated through the hero-worship of younger Templars for older members of the Order, which was encouraged and led to sexual relationships.

Many Templars agreed that they were given permission for sexual relationships with other brothers, but also added that they did not take any action on this, although some said they had done so, or had seen such acts take place. Gilmour-Bryson has analysed evidence from the Italian trials that shows that sodomy did take place, and she concluded that in an all-male society this was inevitable.[18] Sodomy, like heresy, was punishable by burning.

One of the greatest living crusader historians, Professor Jonathan Riley-Smith, entered the debate on the Templars' guilt in 2004. He drew attention to the fact that the trial had different results in different countries. He also made the point that not much reliability can be given to confessions made 'under conditions not conducive to objectivity'. He dismissed the charges that Templars were forbidden to confess to priests outside the Order, and concluded that on the whole the evidence shows that the Templars were orthodox Catholics.[19]

He accepted that illicit kisses took place at the reception, citing the evidence of a hostile witness in England who said that boys would shout 'Beware the kiss of a Templar', and from the French trials evidence that Laurence de Nantes had paled at the thought of kissing the 'scabby stomach' of the brother receiving him. Riley-Smith accepted that homosexuality took place, and that would have been natural in an all-male society. Those who thought it was permitted by the Order had misunderstood the Templar Rule that said that Templars must share their beds when there was a shortage. The idea that the cords the Templars were given had touched an idol was also part of a misunderstanding, as was the fact that many believed that an unordained Templar could give absolution.[20] The Order's obsessive secrecy, however, could not be denied, and reports of the events at the reception, denying Christ and spitting on the cross seem to have been universal except in Britain and Aragon. It would appear that corruption had entered the Order, but on the other hand the denial of Christ could be a symbolic re-enactment of St Peter's denial. Professor Riley-Smith concluded that 'in some commanderies blasphemous demands were being made at the time of, or shortly after, reception into the Order.' Whether or not all the charges were true it was clear that the Knights Templar were in dire need of reform.[21]

Review of the evidence against the Knights Templar

There is a great deal of evidence from the various Knights Templar trials across Europe. In order to make it more manageable this will be presented in the six main categories of the Articles of Accusation.

Reception

The first group concerns the articles about reception into the Order. The accusations stated that the receptions were held in secret without lay persons being present. At the reception the initiate had to deny Christ, and spit, trample or urinate on the image of Christ on the cross. Indecent kisses were exchanged, and the initiate was given a cord to wear under his shirt at all times. The initiate had to swear never to reveal the Order's secrets or to leave the Order without permission. Anyone refusing to do any of these things would be killed or imprisoned.

The majority of the French Templars admitted that at their reception they had been told that Christ was a false prophet, born of man rather than God and unable to offer redemption. They were told they must deny him, and were then shown an image of Christ on the cross and told to spit on it. Indecent kisses on the buttocks, navel and penis as well as on the mouth were exchanged. The initiate was then given a cord which some said had touched an idol to wear under his shirt, to remind him of his chastity.

The English Templars at first denied that any of this happened, although most agreed that the reception was held in secret, usually during the night or at dawn. The apostate Templars described two receptions, one in which the Templar Rule was obeyed and the other where they were forced by knights with drawn swords to deny Christ, and spit on the cross. Once they had confessed this the rest of the English Templars followed their example, and confessed to these things as well. However, William Raven, a knight received at Temple Combe five years before the trial, said that there were a hundred secular people present at his reception. Yet Thomas Chamberlain, received at Faxfleet in Yorkshire eight years earlier, said that when he was received the door of the chapel was locked. William Crawcombe, received at Lidley three years before, said that all the receptions were good, and that there were no bad receptions. The Templars in Aragon denied any wrongdoing at their receptions.[22]

All the Templars were given a white cord to wear under their shirts. This was to remind them of their vow of chastity and if we analyse the timetable of the receptions we can see order in which events took place. First the Templar Rule was explained to the initiate who then vowed to follow it, and never to reveal the Order's secrets or leave the Order. The religious vows of chastity, obedience and poverty were taken after this, and the Temple mantle was placed around the initiate's neck, followed by the kisses of acceptance. It was at this point that the cord was given to the new Templar to remind him of his vow of chastity. It was also at this point (if at all) that the new Templar was told that Christ was a false prophet and an image of Christ on the cross was produced and the initiate told to spit on it. This followed a vow of obedience. Was this a test of obedience? Absolute obedience was essential in a military order. The initiate was being asked to do something that was alien to all his beliefs and the Catholic faith. Would he obey? Some testified that they spat on the ground or on their hand. Others that they were forced to do spit on the cross by fear of what might happen to them if they disobeyed (a good maxim for maintaining military discipline). But the responses may alternatively have been designed to placate their inquisitors and release them from torment.

The events at the reception could be seen as the general horseplay that surrounds initiation ceremonies into all-male societies, including parts of the armed forces, and not necessarily evidence of the Order's corruption. From the evidence it is clear that this sort of reception had been in process for at least 40 years before the arrests. All the Templar high officers would have been through the same process and passed it on.

The Templar Rule describes the reception and how it should take place. It says that after taking his vows the initiate should receive the kiss of acceptance. But Rule No. 11 states that the reception should test the soul to see if it cares for God. The Rule should be read to the initiate to see if he agrees to keep it, and the master and the brothers wish to admit him. Rule 274 gives the formula of the vow of obedience that was made according to canonical institution and 'according to the precept of the Lord'. It continued that a written document should be prepared to the effect that the initiate had promised obedience, chastity and to live without property and to keep the way of life of the brothers of the house and the Knights of Christ.[23]

Any additions to the reception must have been transmitted by example and word of mouth. If all Templars who had taken the vow of obedience were then tested on this it would have helped to consolidate the Order through common experience, and there is no evidence that after the reception any Templar was again asked to deny Christ or spit on the cross again. The Templars were then perhaps guilty of the Articles of Accusation about the reception, but without heretical intent.

Idolatry

The next group of articles concern idolatry. It was claimed that each province possessed an idol which was worshipped at chapter meetings, and which would make the land fertile and the Templars rich. The idol was either in the form of a black cat or a head.

Worship of an idol was against the Ten Commandments ('Thou shalt not worship graven images'). Although medieval churches were stuffed full of the images of saints and their relics, the adoration of an image which could not be identified as a saint was against Church teaching. Furthermore, the description of the idol smacked of paganism, and the introduction of a black cat suggested devil worship and witchery. One Templar examined at Poitiers even said that their idol was a cat, and the devil was a type of cat.[24]

Twenty-eight individual Templars in France claimed to have seen the idol. Four of them claimed it was a cat, the rest that it was a head. A hostile witness in England said it was a golden calf, an obvious Biblical reference.[25] None of the descriptions of the alleged idol tallied exactly, although there was some uniformity of evidence. Most descriptions said it was a head, or the size of a man's head, with a beard and a frightening expression. But it was variously made of metal or wood, or it was an embalmed or mummified head, or it was a human face coloured red, or it stood on four legs, two in the front and two at the back. Another description was of a painted board with an image on it. At the Carcassonne examinations the 'idol' was claimed to be the figure of a man wearing a dalmatic (a priest's robe), and said to be called Baffomet, or Yalla by the Saracens.[26] Robert Courteix, a sergeant who had been in the Order forty years, said he had heard that brothers overseas possessed a head that none had seen called Mandagora.[27]

Stephen de Troyes, a servant of 11 years' standing, said that when he had been received into the Order by Hugues de Pairaud he had seen the idol carried in by a priest accompanied by two Templars carrying lit silver candelabras. The idol was a fleshy head with a black-and-white beard like a Templar's beard, and its neck was encrusted with gold, silver and precious stones. The Templars present had made homage to it with great reverence, and he had heard that it was said to be the head of Hugh de Payens.[28] This last reference is one of the most logical assumptions about the idol to be made by a Templar. It was likely that the Templars would revere the founder of their Order, and may even have had his mummified head.

The mention of Hugues de Pairaud in relation with the idol is interesting as he is the only Templar of high office who was connected in any way to the idol, and one of only three knights who mentioned it, the rest being sergeants or chaplains. Pairaud admitted that he had actually held the idol at a chapter meeting in Montpelier, and it was he who described it as a head on four feet.[29] Other Templars also attested to having seen the idol at Montpelier.[30]

An outside witness, Anthony Syici of Vercellis, who was a public notary, said he believed the idol came from Sidon, and was the head of a noblewoman, a virgin who had been the beloved of a Sidonian lord. She had died before their love could be consummated. After her death the lord had been to her tomb, and had intercourse with her corpse. As he left he was told by a ghostly voice to return in nine months to collect the fruit of his loins. He did this and found the head. The same voice told him to guard the head carefully as it would bring fertility and wealth. Anthony claimed he had been told this tale by Matthew de Saumage of Picardy who had heard it from a soldier in Babylon.[31]

A similar tale was told by a Hugh de Faures, a knight who had been in the Order for 25 years, had served in the East, and had been present at the fall of Acre. He claimed to have heard the story from a secular knight at Limassol in Cyprus. The story went that a damsel in a castle in Tripoli was loved by a nobleman. When he heard she had died he had her exhumed and had intercourse with her, and afterwards cut off her head. When he did this he heard a voice say that whoever saw the head would be destroyed, so he covered the head and hid it in a chest. This nobleman hated the Greeks who were in Cyprus so he took the head to their castle and exposed it so that they would be destroyed. He then went to Constantinople to destroy that city, but on the voyage the key to the chest was stolen by his nurse who wanted to see what was inside it. She opened the chest and a great storm blew up, and sank the ship. But not everyone was lost. The sailors survived to tell the tale, but everyone else perished. He added that he did not know how the head came into the Templars' possession.[32] These two versions about the head have been given in detail because as we shall see later they have a remarkable resemblance to stories told about Mary Magdalene, who plays a continuing part in the Templar legend.

So were the Templars guilty of idolatry? No heads were found when the Templars were arrested, and in France they would not have had time to dispose of these, although it has been suggested that those Templars who escaped took the head(s) with them and hid them elsewhere. What is more likely is that the heads did exist, but these were reliquaries. Many relics were kept in head-shaped containers. This made them easy to transport, and to stand on altars. The variation in descriptions might mean that there were different reliquaries in different Templar chapels.

One French Templar suggested the head was female and that it contained bones, and it has been suggested that the head was one of the 11,000 virgin martyrs of Cologne. But if it was a reliquary why did some of the witnesses suggest that it had a Muslim origin? Most of the witnesses describing the head were sergeants or servants, unlettered men who may never have travelled far, but knew that the Templars originated in the East where they had fought against the Saracens. This may be a case of a little knowledge being transformed into actual fact. It is also a tribute to the power of suggestion. We do not know what the inquisitors suggested to those they were interrogating . The inquisitors' task was to find the Templars guilty and condemn them. Confessions of idolatry and occult practices would do nicely.

The verdict on whether the Templars worshipped idols or not is therefore 'not guilty'.

Heresy

The third group of articles concerned denying Christ as a false prophet, refusing to believe in the sacrament, and if celebrating mass in an outside church not looking at the host when it was raised by the priest. The beliefs that the master, who was not an ordained priest, could give absolution, and that Templars could confess to their colleagues who were not ordained represented, as far as the Church was concerned, the most important clutch of accusations. These hit at the heart of the Christian faith and the institution of the Catholic Church, which taught that only an ordained priest could mediate between the sinner and God. This was the major objection to medieval heretical movements such as the Cathars or the Albigensians who allowed lay people, men and women, to talk directly to God.

The denial of Christ was said to have taken place at the reception and may in fact have been a test for the initiate. So many Templars admitted to it that it almost certainly happened. However, the accusation that they did not believe in the sacrament and acted accordingly was denied by most. Jacques de Molay said in his retraction that the Knights Templar were practising Catholics. So-called hostile witnesses confirmed this. Lord John Baudin said of the Templars in Cyprus that he had heard mass in their house at Limassol and had seen them take the host as other Christians do. Lord John Mountolive, also from Cyprus, said that the Templars were devoted Christians.[33]

The Templars who admitted that an non-ordained member of the Order could hear confessions and give absolution had probably misunderstood what happened at chapter meetings, or what they were being asked by the inquisitors. At a chapter meeting a Templar could confess to sins against the Order or another brother, and be given a penance or punishment and be absolved by the preceptor. This was not a sacramental absolution, but a public confession of errors and omissions, which was the normal practice in monastic houses. The Church was aware that this happened in all the military orders, and in the late twelfth century it had been described as a 'wilful intrusion of priestly functions'.[34] But the Templar Rule described how the confession and subsequent penance should be dealt with in some detail.

Confession to a fellow Templar who was not ordained may have happened in practice as the ratio of ordained priests to the rest was low. When *in extremis* in the time of war it may have been necessary to confess to a non-ordained fellow Templar in order to receive absolution in case of death. The chaos of the siege of Acre would be an example of this, as many lay dying and the task of absolving them stretched the resources of the priests and chaplains.

The Templars were probably not guilty of heretical practices, but they were confused Catholics, and their attitude to absolution put them in the same position as other non-conformist religious sects.

Immorality

The next group of articles deals with immorality. Like the convicted heretic, the convicted sodomite could be punished by being burnt to death at the stake. The Articles of Accusation accused the Templars of exchanging carnal kisses at their reception, of being given permission to have sexual relations with each other, and of actually carrying this out.

A number of French Templars admitted to having received carnal kisses at their reception; sometimes on the base of the spine, the navel and the penis, as well as on the mouth. Jean de Cugy, examined in Paris, who had been received by Hugues de Pairaud nine years earlier, said he was first kissed on the mouth, second on the base of the spine (buttock?) and third on the navel.[35] Of 225 Templars examined before the papal commissioners in Paris 100 admitted to receiving carnal kisses at their reception, and 71 said they had been given permission for sexual relationships with other Templars.[36] The Templar Rule, statute 418, explicitly condemned sodomy.

One Templar described what might have been a homosexual act at his reception. William de Bon, knight said that he had been laid on the ground with hands and feet outstretched during his reception.[37] On the other hand this may have been a form of prostration as a sinner. At Carcassonne Jean Cassan, a knight received 28 years earlier at the age of 22, said that at his reception he was placed face down on a bench and brother John kissed his anus.[38] Templar Statute 274 on the reception described what should happen. After the vows were taken the initiate should lie across the altar and prostrate himself and say 'Receive me, Lord, in accordance with your way and let me live.' This was followed by prayers.[39] What happened at Carcassonne, according to Cassan, was an obvious perversion of this, which suggests that the Order had become corrupt, at least in some of its houses.

Some Templar witnesses said they had seen sexual acts between Templars. One, Hugh de Narsac, preceptor of Espans, even accused Jacques de Molay of having relations with his personal valet George. Poor George, Narsac added, was later drowned for his sins.[40] Robert Courteix, a sergeant, admitted having sexual relationships with three brothers, and Stephen de Tours said that he remembered being approached by Paul de Valleceli to have sexual relations with him, and when he refused he was beaten up. When he complained about this treatment at a chapter meeting he was told that sexual relations between Templars was permitted, and he should have submitted.[41]

The Order was well aware that homosexuality existed within it. Examples of crimes within the Order for which punishment was given were added to the Rule some time between 1252 and 1267. One instance was at Castle Pelerin in the Holy Land where there were three brothers who practised 'wicked sin' and caressed each other in their chambers at night. Those who knew about this and had suffered from it reported it to the master who on the advice of the chapter decided that this was so distasteful that the offenders should be sent to the Templar headquarters at Acre, and be put in irons. One of those involved, Lucas, escaped and defected to the Saracens. Another tried to escape but was killed, the third was imprisoned for a long time.[42]

So it would appear that homosexuality was endemic in the Order, and the Order dealt with it in its own way. The reference to the Templar who defected to the Saracens was part of the Christian myth that the Saracens condoned homosexuality as part of their culture. But as far as Christians were concerned sodomy was condemned in the Bible as a waste of seed, and it should be destroyed like Sodom city in the Old Testament. In the New Testament homosexuality was described by St Paul in the first epistle to the Romans as unseemly. By the eleventh century homosexual acts had to be confessed as a sin, but conversely twelfth-century literary works extolled male beauty and platonic male friendships.[43] It was with the advent of the Inquisition that society became less tolerant and homosexuals became the scapegoat for other evils and classed with heretics. Accusations against heretics usually included the charge of heresy.

In an all-male institutions such as the Knights Templar homosexuality was probably inevitable. However, the Templars had taken vows of chastity and wore a cord to remind themselves of this, and the Rule said they were to sleep in their clothes with the lights on to prevent any immorality. Ironically many of the folk tales told about Templars referred to their womanizing. It was said that a woman was not a woman until she had been with a Templar, and the same section of the Rule that described crimes for which a penance and punishment were required included the punishment of a brother who slept with a woman.[44] Undoubtedly some Templars were guilty of sodomy. But they were victims of an intolerant society that condemned them.

Charity and wealth

The penultimate group of articles concerned the charity given by the Templars. It was claimed that the Templars did not offer hospitality as in other religious houses, and that they acquired their wealth by illegal means. The accusation of not offering hospitality was unfair as the Templars had been set up to protect pilgrims and not give them lodging. Moreover, according to the evidence from Cyprus they did infact give lodging to men, and alms to the poor. This is corroborated by evidence from England which however indicates that when alms were given this was done in such a way as to make the poor as undignified as possible.[45] Some French Templars testified that their preceptories gave alms and hospitality.[46] It seems that whether hospitality and alms were given depended on the individual commandery and master.

One of the tales told about the alleged idol was that it brought the Templars great riches. There is no evidence that they obtained wealth by illegal means, although they may have brought pressure to bear on potential donors by suggesting that a gift to them could release their souls from Purgatory. Many of the grants of land state in their preamble that these were given for the health of the soul of the donor, his or her family, parents and ancestors. But this was the normal form of words used when donating a property to a religious house. The Rheims obit roll, a list of donors and what they gave the Templars, shows how this worked. On the anniversary of the donor's death masses were said for his or her soul to speed it to heaven. The Rheims roll is a rare survival, but similar documents must have existed elsewhere.

The Templars' fabled wealth turned out to be just that – a fable. They had no great riches, but were as they claimed the poor knights of the Temple of Solomon. The cartloads of cash and jewels seen going into the Paris and London Temples did not belong to them, but were being deposited for safekeeping. The bulk of their income was ploughed back into their efforts to maintain a foothold for Christendom in the Holy Land.

Secrecy

The final group of articles concerned the Order's extreme secrecy. It appears to be fact that they held their chapter meetings at night behind locked doors, and receptions of new members took place either at midnight or at dawn. Himbert Blank from the Auvergne who was arrested in England suggested that it was the Templars' secrecy that had been their downfall.[47]

It could be argued that what went on behind closed doors in the Templar houses was their business alone. If they chose to hold their meetings at unsociable hours that was up to them. But such secrecy was viewed with suspicion in the fourteenth century. Secret meetings could be seen as agents of subversion plotting religious, political or social revolution. Such meetings had the taint of occult and witchcraft about them, which was threatening to the fabric of society. This was one reason that the Knights Templar had to be eradicated, for secrecy was a crime.

Whether the evidence showed them to be guilty or not the Knights Templar were abolished. But was there another ideological reason for the suppression of the Order at this particular time? Menarche suggested that they had failed in the eyes of their contemporaries by not living up to the expectations of knightly conduct. Professor Riley-Smith argued that the Order was in terminal decline and in need of reform.[48]

Of course, the Templars had been attracting accusations almost since their foundation. As we have seen, when things went wrong in battle or at a siege the chroniclers blamed the Templars. They were accused of betraying Christians to the enemy, of avarice and pride and contributing to the loss of the Holy Land through their greed. The fact that they did not pay tithes or local taxes added to their unpopularity, and their lack of allegiance to any one western prince or state created suspicion. But the accusations levelled against them went beyond mere jealousy and hit at their ideals, their Catholic faith and their morals. They were guilty of some of the accusations, but they were also victims of a French king who for political, economic and religious reasons wanted rid of them, and of a leader of the Church who failed to prevent this happening.

G.R. Wilkins suggests that author of *Sir Gawain and the Green Knight*, an anonymous poet of the fourteenth century, portrays Sir Gawain as a symbol of the last vestiges of religious knighthood. Interestingly, the Green Knight was represented by a disembodied head, itself, it turns out, a symbol of the fall of the Templars.[49]

Notes

1 E. Lord, *The Knights Templar in Britain*, London: Pearson Education (2004), p. 265.

2 Lord, p. 264.

3 Lord, p. 268.

4 Lord, p. 268.

5 Lord, p. 268.

6 J. von Hammer-Purgstall, *Die Schuld der Templier*, Vienna: Akad der Wissenschaft (1853); J. Prutz, *Entwicklung und Untergang des Tempelherorden*, Berlin: G. Groesch Verlagbuch (1888).

7 C.G. Addison, *The History of the Knights Templar*, London: Longman (2nd ed.1842).

8 Justice Shallow, undated MS in Cambridge University History.

9 J.G. Morshead, *The Templar Trials*, London: Stevens & Son (1888), p. 53.

10 Morshead, p. 76.

11 Morshead, p. 77.

12 Justice Shallow, alias J.G. Morshead, *Conjectures on the Templars' Process*, CUL Syn 4.91.47 (1918), pp. 1, 4, 6, 36.

13 E. Martin, *The Trial of the Templars*, London: Allen & Unwin (1928), pp. 33, 62.

14 E. Peters, *The Magician, the Witch and the Law*, Philadelphia: University of Pennsylvania Press (1978), pp. 125, 127–8.

15 M. Barber, *The New Knighthood*, Cambridge: CUP (1993), pp. 295, 301.

16 M. Barber, *The Trial of the Templars*, Cambridge: CUP (1993), pp. 244–6.

17 M. Barber, 'Propaganda in the Middle Ages: The Charges Against the Templars', *Nottingham Medieval Studies*, vol. XVII (1973), pp. 42–57; Peters writes that 'Barber's conclusion about general magic and witchcraft are not be trusted', Peters, p. 137.

18 A. Gilmour-Bryson, 'Sodomy and the Knights Templar', *Journal of the History of Sexuality*, vol. 7, no. 2 (1996), pp. 151–83.

19 J. Riley-Smith, 'Were the Templars Guilty?' in S. Ridgard (ed.), *The Medieval Crusade*, Woodbridge, Boydell Press (2004), pp. 109, 112–3.

20 Riley-Smith, pp. 113–14.

21 Riley-Smith, pp. 117, 121, 214.

22 D.C. Wilkins, *Concilia Magnae Britannaie*, London (1737), pp. 334–5, 341.

23 J. Upton-Ward, *The Templar Rule*, Woodbridge: Boydell Press (1992), pp. 22, 80–1.

24 H. Finke, *Papsstum und Untergang des Templeorden* II, Munster: Druck und Verlag des Aschendorffer Buchandlung (1907), p. 350.

25 When Moses came down the mountain after receiving the tablets of the Law he found the Israelites worshipping a golden calf.

26 Finke, pp. 313–63.

27 R. Sève, and A.M. Chagny-Sève, *Le Procès des Templiers d'Auvergne*, Paris: Editions du CTHS (1986), p. 214.

28 Finke, p. 335.

29 J. Michelet, *Le Procès des Templiers* II, Paris: Les Editions du CTHS (1987), p. 363.

30 Finke, p. 335.

31 Michelet II, p. 645.

32 Michelet II, pp. 223–4.

33 A. Gilmour-Bryson, *The Trial of the Templars in Cyprus*, Leiden: Brill (1998), pp. 57–8.

34 H.C. Lea, *Minor Historical Writings*, Philadelphia: University of Pennsylvania (1942), pp. 97–9.

35 Michelet II, pp. 306–7.

36 Morshead, pp. 77–9.

37 R. Sève, and A.M. Chagny-Sève, p. 148.

38 Finke II, p. 322.

39 Upton-Ward, p. 276.

40 Michelet II, p. 208.

41 Sève, p. 214; Finke, p. 335.

42 Upton-Ward, p. 573

43 J. Boswell, *Christianity, Social Tolerance and Homosexuality*, Chicago: Chicago University Press (1980), pp. 194, 213, 233.

44 Upton-Ward, p. 160.

45 Wilkins, pp. 333–4.

46 Michelet I, p. 192.

47 Wilkins, p. 338.

48 S. Menarche, 'The Templar Order: A Failed Ideal?' *Catholic Historical Review*, vol. LXXIX (1993), p. 2; Riley-Smith, 'Were the Templars Guilty?

49 G.R. Wilkins, 'The Dissolution of the Templar Ideal in Sir Gawain and the Green Knight', *English Studies* (1982), pp. 63, 113–14.

CHAPTER 14

· · · · · · · · · · · · · · ·

Who were the
Knights Templar?

Although there are scattered references to individual Templars before the trials, and of course full lists of Grand Masters and most provincial masters, it is not until the arrests and the trials that we get an almost complete list of all the membership. The trial proceedings give some indication of their age when entering the Order and their age when tried. Other information can be put together in order to examine their background, family and origins, but of necessity much of this reconstruction is speculative. As individuals the Templars had some elements in common. They had to be freemen rather than servile. They had to be healthy and unmarried, or if they had been married they needed permission from their wives to join the Templars. They had to be free from debt. This much we know from the Templar Rule. It can also be assumed that they were the younger sons of freemen, especially those who came from armorial-bearing landed families since the eldest son would inherit an estate and be responsible for continuing the dynasty. The Knights Templar were active during the period when European landed families were developing the system of primogeniture in which the land passed down the same blood line through the eldest male heir, and was continued by his, hopefully advantageous marriage. It was unlikely that the heir was going to be allowed by his family to join an order of monkish knights who took a vow of chastity.

The sergeants probably came from the section of society that later became known as the yeomen or the gentry; substantial freemen possessing freehold land. Again they were probably younger sons. Despite not wishing to lose the heir, the families from whom the Templars came would have considered it an honour to dedicate one of their sons to God in this way. There is some evidence that there were 'Templar families' who supplied more than one member. In France there were the Pairauds, uncle and nephew, in England the Sautres, again probably uncle and nephew, the Stretchs and the Tanets.

Malcolm Barber describes the first Templars as 'pious laymen seeking an outlet for their religious impulses.' They joined the Order to 'channel the war-like aspects of the ruling class into Christian understanding, and impose moral restraint on the knightly class'. Barber estimates that to equip and support a knight needed an estate of 150 hectares.[1] We do not know if on entering the Order they bought their own equipment with them, but often there was a gift of land or other property from the family.

If the Templar Knights were well connected with the ruling elites of Europe, why did none of their connections attempt to help them when they were arrested? No French nobleman or senior churchman raised a force to rescue a family member or friend or even spoke up in the Templars' favour. No one stepped forward to save Jacques de Molay or Geoffroi de Charney from being burnt, even though the latter probably had high-born relatives in Normandy. In England the families who had donated land to the Templars in the first place scrambled to repossess it. Is this evidence of the Templars' general unpopularity, and a kind of crusading fatigue in the West? Was the Order really in terminal decline, and how many members did it have to support it?

How many Knights Templar were there?

The actual number of Knights Templar will never be known. Clearly there were more Knights when they were on active service in the East, than in the last decades of the Order when they had withdrawn to the West. In their early days they needed a constant supply of men to replace those lost in battle and to disease. At least 300 Templars were killed in the same year at the Springs of Cresson and the Horns of Hattin. Immediately prior to Hattin, Barber estimates that there were about 600 knights, 2,000 sergeants and 50 chaplains in the East. In the West he estimates there were two to three Templars in each of their houses. The evidence he gives for this comes from the cartulary of Richerenches in France, which suggests that there were 10 Templars in 1138, 20 in 1163 and 18 in 1180. There were also eight dependent houses each with three resident Templars,[2] making a total of 42 Templars in that area. By the time of the arrests Barber suggests there were 970 houses and about 7,000 Templars, their employees and their families.[3] The staff in these houses far outnumbered the Templars themselves, and the number of actual Templars in Europe in 1307 was probably, as a general estimate, 2,000.

Forey gives a figure of about 200 Templars in Aragon, of whom only 150 can be traced, and 84 of whom were still living in 1319.[4] Other estimates of the number of Templars in 1307 vary from 5,000 to 20,000.[5] The latter figure seems wide of the mark. But we do not know how many escaped arrest, and how many died in prison before coming to trial. The total number tried was about 1,153 individuals.[6] So a conservative estimate would in indeed be about 2,000 in total, knights, sergeants and chaplains. The sources available for an estimation of the population of the period are scarce. Werner Rosener suggests that in 1300 England may have had a population of about 4.5 million, France 21 million and Germany 14 million.[7] The Knights Templar were, therefore, only a small proportion of the total population. However, the amount of land they held was disproportionate to their numbers, and land meant revenues and power, putting the Knights Templar on a par with the aristocracy.

Templar demography

When the Templars were active in the Holy Land their ideal recruit was young, fit and trained to arms, and would have been sent, like Jacques de Molay, out to the East soon after being received into the Order. He would have been withdrawn to the West at intervals, and Templars who survived the battles, heat and disease were eventually given an honourable retirement at places like Denny Abbey in Cambridgeshire or Eagle in Lincolnshire.

To join the Order the recruit had to be an adult aged 18 or 20 years, although some were younger, and others much older. As we have seen, at the trial they were asked how many years had elapsed since they were

TABLE 14.1 ◆ *Estimate of the Ages of Templars on joining the Order as a rounded percentage of those tried*

Age	Paris (%)	Aragon (%)	Auvergne (%)	Britain (%)
Under 20	3	25	1	4
20–29	21	43	27	35
30–39	16	24	17	19
40–49	19	4	27	24
50–59	25	3	20	11
60–69	12	40	20	7
70+	3	<1	8	<1

received into the Order. From this figure we can make a rough estimate of how old they might have been when they joined (see Table 14.1).

Jacques de Molay had been in the Order 42 years, so he was at least 60 when he was arrested. Geoffroi de Charney, who faced death with him, was the same age. Both spent seven years in prison, and would have been approaching 70 when they were burnt at the stake. Over half the Templars in Britain were under 40 when received, and this seems to have been the pattern elsewhere.

William de la More was probably in his fifties when he was arrested. One unfortunate had only been in the Order for 11 days when he was arrested, and three more had been members for little more than a year. The relative youth of many of those tried meant they were facing a long term of punishment when they were sent to monasteries to do penance individually for the Order's collective sins.

The social background of the Templars

Individual social background was reflected in the position a Templar held in the hierarchy of the Order. Knights were likely to come from knightly families, and sergeants from lower down the social scale. The Grand Masters were usually of French origin, although at least one, Philip of Nablus (1169–71), must have been born in the East; Gerard de Ridefort (1185–9) may have been of from an English or Irish family; while William de Beaujeu (1273–91) was the fourth son of a noble family related to Charles of Anjou and the French royal family.[8]

Provincial masters also came from arm-bearing families. In England the first master was Hugh Argentine (1140) who came from a family with large estates in Hertfordshire; Richard de Hastings (1155–64) came from a noble family who were to be confidants of kings throughout the middle ages, eventually becoming the Earls of Huntingdon; and Alan Martel (1218–25) also had illustrious relatives.

Brian de Jay and William de la More may have shared a background on the Welsh marches in Shropshire. The addition of 'de' to a name denoted the place of origin of the family, where they held their main estates. Jay was a village in Shropshire where a knightly family of the same name held a manor.[9] La More was also a village in Shropshire where a family of the same name were landlords.[10] It is probable that the family of another English Templar, William de la Forde, also derived from Shropshire.[11] Other English Templars who came from noble families included Thomas Chamberlain, whose family was of Norman origin, John Moun or Mohun, Richard Peitevin or Poitevein, Philip Mewes or Meaux from the North Cave area of Yorkshire, John Coffin who came from a prominent Devonshire family, and Thomas Tocci who may have been a member of the Tuchet family.[12]

Rank-and-file Templars are more difficult to trace. Their family names are also often locative names taken from the place where they lived. However, many of these names are ambiguous as there is more than one place with the same name, for example Barton, Chesterton, Stoke or Thorpe. It might be assumed that these Templars would have been received at the nearest preceptory to the town or village they came from, but matching records between likely place of origin and where a person was received as a Knight Templar shows no relationship, as most English receptions took place at a provincial council, usually held at Dinsley in Hertfordshire. But from the little information we have it is possible to provide some life-histories of the Templars who came to trial.

Templar biographies

One of the rank-and-file Templars about whom most is known is the Templar of Tyre, who left a chronicle describing the last days of the Templars in Syria, the fall of Acre and the exile to Cyprus. He was

William de Beaujeu's secretary and so was present at all the great events affecting the Templars in their final years. We do not know his full name, but we know he was born in Tyre and spent his early years there. His chronicle starts in 1241, but since he first appears in other documents in 1269 aged 15 and serving as a page to Marguerite de Montfort, and he claimed to have been 55 in 1309, his birth date can be assumed to be 1254, and he must have started his chronicle with events that he had not witnessed himself. He stayed in Tyre until 1273 when he went to Acre, arriving there at the same time as William de Beaujeu who had just been elected Grand Master. From 1273 onwards he served Beaujeu and on Beaujeu's death his successor Thibaut Gaudin. He records his desolation at having to leave the Holy Land for Cyprus. He was in Cyprus in 1303 when Henry II of Cyprus was deposed by Amaury de Lusignan with the connivance of the Templars. He did not appear amongst the Templars interrogated in Cyprus, and the end of the chronicle is incomplete.[13] The career of the Templar of Tyre exemplifies the careers open to boys in a noble household. Educated either by a tutor or at monastic schools and then sent away to serve in another aristocratic household, their subsequent life-choice's were between a return to the family estate, pursuit of public office or membership of a religious foundation.

Michel Miguet has compiled short biographies for 25 Templars from Normandy, using information from the trials about where and when they were received into the Order, by whom and who was present at the time, their rank, receptions of others they witnessed and where they were tried.[14] For example: Philip Agate, commander of St Vauborg, aged 60 in 1311, was received in 1281 at Bourgault, which implies that he was 60 when he was received into the Order. He witnessed a number of receptions himself, and was tried at Caen.

The longest-serving Templar in Englands was Thomas of Tholosa or Toulouse, a knight. At the time of the trial he had been in the order for 42 years, and would have been in his sixties by the time of the arrests, and approaching 70 when he was tried. He was received into the Order at Dinsley in Hertfordshire by Himbert Pairaud. Present were William de la Forde and Richard Peitevin who were probably all received at the same ceremony, as Thomas recalled witnessing their receptions. In all Thomas was present at 20 receptions at least, mostly in the Canterbury archdiocese, and including that of the apostate Stephen Staplebridge.

Had Thomas ever served abroad? There is no actual record of this, but there is a gap of ten years between Thomas being received and the next reception he witnessed, so that he could have been in the East between *c.*1267 and *c.*1277. This would be a logical assumption as he would have been young and fit at that time, and an ideal candidate to carry arms into the field. He was back in England in 1277 when he witnessed the reception of William Grafton in London. William Grafton became the chief Templar in the north, and he officiated at or witnessed most receptions in the archdiocese of York.

By the time of the arrests Thomas was commander of Upleden in Hertfordshire, where the other resident Templar was Thomas Chamberlain, whose reception Thomas had witnessed at Faxfleet in Yorkshire, a rare visit north for him. It is probable that Thomas died whilst imprisoned in the Tower of London, for he disappears from the records before the Templars were allocated to monasteries.

The shortest-serving Templar at the time of the trials was Thomas de Ludham, who had been received into the Order at Temple Ewell in Kent only 11 days before the arrests. William de la More officiated and present were Ralph Barton, the priest from the New Temple in London, Himbert Blanke from the Auvergne and many others. Thomas de Ludham may have come from Ludham in Norfolk, but little else is known about him.

Stephen de Staplebridge, who condemned the Order by confessing to two receptions, a good and a bad, was probably in his thirties at the time of his arrest. He had been received into the Order at Dinsley 11 years earlier by Brian de Jay (and if we are looking for a 'bad' master in England it has to be Brian de Jay who was eventually killed fighting the Scots, shedding Christian blood in direct contradiction to the Order's Rule and Christian precepts). Present at Staplebridge's reception were Thomas of Tholosa, Richard de Herdwick, Ralph Malton the carpenter, and Thomas Tocci of Thoroldeby. As Stephen's name is given as 'de' or 'of' Staplebridge this appears to refer to a place. But which place is debatable. Stephen observed four other receptions.

Such sketchy biographies of the English Templars who faced trial can be reproduced for most of them, but they do not give much information about each one, nor do they tell us what they were like as men, their motivation for joining the Order, or their reaction to the arrests and subsequent trial.

Not all English Templars, however, were in England at the time of the arrests, and at least one was burnt to death in France.

English Templars abroad

The first group to be discussed are Templars who were in England at the time of their arrests but had served abroad. The most notable of these was Robert Scot, who had joined the Order in the East and had subsequently left, possibly because of a disagreement with Himbert Blanke. After a period outside the Order he decided to re-join and had travelled to Rome to be absolved for his apostasy by the pope, and had rejoined the Order at Nicosia in Cyprus where he and Himbert Blanke were reconciled. From Cyprus he returned to England and was arrested at the Templar hospital at Denny in Cambridgeshire.[15]

In the East at the same time as Robert Scot was William Winchester. He had been received by William de Beaujeu 26 years earlier at Castle de la Roca in Armenia. He may be the same William who had been present at the reception of Peter of Tripoli in Armenia, 22 years before the trial. So he had probably been in the East for at least four years. John de Stoke had been received into the Order in Picardy, and Ralph de Roston, a priest, in Cyprus.[16] All of these were in England when they were arrested.

The second group are those English Templars who were abroad at the time of the arrests. One of these was Richard Grafton, whom Richard Collingham informed the commissioners was in Cyprus. He may be the priest and chaplain referred to in the Cypriot trials. Another English Templar in Cyprus was a sergeant called John who had originally been received in Italy.[17] Evidence from the trial in Cyprus includes two knights who were received in England but may not have been English. Hugh de Mali was received in England by William de la More at a place called in 'Meca' four years earlier;[18] present were Richard the English chaplain, and Philip Mewes. Stephen Mally of Burgundy had also been received in England five years previously at Dinsley by William de la More, and in the presence of Thomas of Tholosa and William Grafton.[19] A French Templar who had been received in England was Geoffrey de Gonville, knight and preceptor of Aquitaine who had been received by Robert Turville in London 28 years previously.[20]

A number of English Templars appear in French trials. One was John the Englishman of 'Hinquemet' (Hinxworth in Hertfordshire perhaps) who had been received at Rouen 36 years earlier. Roger Anglicum may have been another Englishman in France, and John Scot may have come from Scotland.[21]

The evidence of the French Templars who were received in England was vastly different from that of their English counterparts. Gonville described in detail how he was shown the image of Christ on the cross in a missal and told to deny Christ and defile his image. He was afraid to do this and said 'Ha, Lord what shall I do', and they said to him he must be courageous. 'I swore by my life that none would prejudice my soul.' He added that this practice had been introduced by a bad master who had been imprisoned by the sultan and had purchased his freedom by agreeing that in future the Knights Templar would deny Christ. He believed that there had been members of the English royal family present at his reception, and some who had done great service in the royal council in England.[22]

A French Templar in England at the time of the arrests was Himbert Blanke, the preceptor of the Auvergne and the Templar visitor who inspected Templar provincial houses. He was fortunate to have been in England at this time, as he was spared the torture and fiery deaths of his French brethren.

The spread of Templars into countries other than that of their origin reflects the international nature of the Order. The evidence we have does not however usually fill in the years between a Templar's reception and his arrest. If we possessed this evidence we would probably see a greater number who had moved between preceptories and crossed national borders. Unfortunately most Templars exist for us only in name and as shadowy figures, many of whom died for their beliefs.

Notes

1 M. Barber, *Crusaders and Heretics 11ᵗʰ to 14ᵗʰ centuries*, Aldershot: Variorum, vol. VIII (1995), pp. 26, 40, 43. This book is a collection of papers published elsewhere and does not have consecutive page numbers but keeps to the numeration of the original paper.

2 Barber XII, p. 319.

3 Barber XII, p. 317.

4 A. Forey, *The Fall of the Templars in the Crown of Aragon*, Aldershot: Ashgate (2001), p. 17.

5 A. Gilmour-Bryson, *The Trial of the Templars in the Papal States and the Abruzzi*, Vatican City: Biblioteca Apostolica Vaticana (1982), p. 10.

6 Gilmour-Bryson, pp. 55–6.

7 W. Rosener, *Peasants in the Middle Ages*, Oxford: Polity Press (1992), p. 34.

8 M. Barber, *The New Knighthood*, Cambridge: CUP (1995), pp. 139, 169.

9 E. Lord, *The Knights Templar in Britain*, London: Pearson Education (2004), p. 188.

10 *Calendar of Inquisitions Post Mortem*, vol. 1, London: HMSO (1904), p. 94.

11 *Inquisitions Post Mortem*, vol. VI (1910), p. 101.

12 G.J. Brand, *Roll of Arms of Edward I (1272–1307)*, Woodbridge: Boydell Press (1997).

13 G. Raynaurd (ed.) *Les Gestes des Chiprois*, Geneva: Jules-Guillaume Fick, *xv–xxvi* (1887), pp. 141–333.

14 M. Miguet, *Templiers et Hospitaliers en Normandie*, Paris: Comité des Travauz Historiques et Scientifiques (1995), p. 134.

15 D.C. Wilkins, *Concilia Magnae Britannae* London (1737), p. 366.

16 Wilkins, pp. 344, 372; A. Gilmour-Bryson, *The Trial of the Templars in Cyprus*, Leiden: Brill (1998), pp. 87–8, 96, 136.

17 Wilkins, p. 341; Gilmour-Bryson, pp. 107, 235, 258.

18 A cedilla makes the 'c' into 'ç', with an s – sound, so the place could have been Masham.

19 Gilmour-Bryson, pp. 87–8, 96.

20 J. Michelet, *Le Procès des Templiers*, Paris: Minstère de l'Education National, vol. II (1987), p. 398.

21 Michelet I, p. 450; II, pp. 132, 398.

22 Michelet II, pp. 398–9.

CHAPTER 15

* * * * * * * * * * * * * * *

The Templar legend

It did not take long after the suppression of the Order and the burning of Jacques de Molay for the Templars to pass into legend. Some of the legends and stories attached to them are related to, and grew out of, evidence given at the trial; others have become grafted onto the Templars through speculation and the vivid imaginations of authors. The secrecy in which the Templars conducted their business, the aura of mystery surrounding them and the unexplained (to fourteenth-century minds) deaths of Clement V and Philip IV following soon after the execution of Jacques de Molay all encouraged speculation, whilst rumours circulated that Philip IV had been murdered by magical means,[1] rumours which led back to the Templars and the charges levelled against them.

Legends attached to the trial evidence and the mediaeval perception of the Templars, were followed by other legends, and the legends are as potent and intriguing today as they have ever been.

The Templar legend and evidence from the trial – the head

The confession by some Knights Templar at their trials that they worshipped an idol in the form of a head, has led to much speculation as to what this could be. The 'idol' was most likely a reliquary in the shape of a head, but some Templars did not recognize it as such. Some said it was called Baphomet (Baffomet) or Yalla by the Saracens, and one suggested that it was known as Mandragora. The name Baphomet was probably a corruption of Muhammad, although it has been suggested that the word might come from the Greek word 'sophia' or wisdom. Yalla was surely a corruption of Allah.[2] Mandragora (common name: mandrake) is a poisonous plant; indeed the name comes probably means 'harmful to cattle'. The yellow fruit was often known as Satan's Apple, and in the middle ages it was used medically as an analgesic, as it numbs the senses when taken with alcohol.[3]

The evidence given at the trial suggested to the commissioners that the idol was of Islamic origin, and convinced them that the Knights Templar had secretly converted to Islam. Some Templars at the French trial reported rumours that a Grand Master had been captured by a sultan, and had purchased his freedom by converting to Islam, and promising that in the future the Knights Templar would deny Christ. This tale was probably the result of half-understood knowledge by Templars in the West about Templar activity in the East, and especially about William de Beaujeu's policy of conciliation with the Muslims. It might also have resulted from a desire by those being tortured to placate their tormentors, but undoubtedly some Templars did make compromises if captured. Malcolm Barber starts his book *The New Knighthood* with the example of two French Templars captured at the siege of Acre in 1291, and discovered in 1340 at the Dead Sea by a German priest. They had survived by working for the sultan, and had married Islamic women and had children by them. When they encountered the stranger from the West it became clear that they had no idea that their Grand Master had been burnt at the stake, or their Order dissolved. Eventually they and their families were repatriated to France.[4]

In some Templar minds the idol in the form of a head seems to have become jumbled up with stories about a necrophiliac prince and a head which would bring fertility to the land and riches to whoever possessed it (see Chapter 13, page 137, for a discussion on this and a summary of the story of the prince). This in turn has become mixed up with Celtic legends such as the magical severed head of Bran the Blessed in *the Mabinogian*, or with legends of a grail where the heads of a king, and a queen, or Adam and Eve were sealed in gold and silver and stored with other heads. According to the legend the golden heads represented the New Law of Christ, and those sealed in silver the false law of the Saracens.[5] The sealed heads are an adaptation of the grail quest called *Perlesvaus* (Perceval) in which the grail castle was conquered by a knight bearing a shield with a red cross. Thus in this legend, the grail, the head and the Templars come together.

The word Baphomet was seized upon and elaborated by Joseph Hammer-Purgstall in *Mysterium Baphomet Revelation*, published in 1818. In this book he suggested that Baphomet was the father of wisdom, and the symbol of a pre-Christian and pre-Muslim cult that flourished in Egypt, and was based on a search to gain all knowledge. This developed into the Gnostic sect, and by extrapolation this must mean that the Knights Templar were Gnostics. As we shall see, speculations about the blood-line of Christ, so skilfully exploited by a twentieth-century novelist, come from the Gnostic Gospel of Philip, so this ties in nicely with the Templars, the head and the grail legend.

In 1855 Eliaphas Levi (alias Alphonse Constant), endowed the head with occult powers. He transposed the idea of the black-and-white Templar banner, representing good and evil, on to the head, and drew two heads placed on a black-and-white diamond. The white head was the bearded head of Christ and the black head that of the Devil.[6] The idea that the Templars' head represented good and evil was continued by Jules Loiseleur in *La Doctrine Secret des Templiers*, published in 1872. His rationale for the head was that it showed that the Templars were a heretical group with beliefs based on the Bogomils, an eleventh-century sect which had developed round the heretical teaching of a tenth-century priest in Bulgaria. The latter preached the dualist nature of life in which good was represented by the Christ figure, and evil by the figure of Satan.[7]

The Bogomils' doctrine was an attempt to explain something that has puzzled Christians for centuries. Why had a good God who created the world allowed evil into it? Why did He allow 'Man's inhumanity to Man', wars and natural disasters to occur? According to the Bogomils these were the work of Satan acting on human beings and nature, and humanity would only be redeemed and saved from these evils by reform and by living a pure and chaste life that excluded Satan. The Bogomils' ideas were remarkably similar to those of St Bernard of Clairvaux, the Templars' patron, and to dualist ideas that influenced the heretical sect the Cathars.

Loisleur went further and suggested that the Knights Templar were a break-away Bogomils sect called the 'Luciferans' who were the representations of Satan on earth, and worshipped the devil instead of God.

Subsequent work by historians has shown that the Luciferans were an imaginary sect, dreamt up by Conrad of Marburg in the fourteenth century in order to condemn troublemakers on his lands.[8] The Templar heads have also been used to suggest that the Templars were Manicheans. Manicheans were members of an eclectic sect, condemned as heretics by the Church, who thought that human beings could achieve perfection only by withdrawal from the world and its temptations.[9]

The idea of the head being something other than a reliquary has been taken further using the descriptions given at the trials of the idol being painted with two feet at the front and two at the back, and another that it was a man in a dalmatic (a priest's robe). These descriptions could be made to match the figure on the Turin Shroud, and it has been suggested that the Templars once had this in their possession. When the shroud reappeared to public view it was in the possession of the de Charney family, and it was a Geoffroi de Charney who died in the flames with Jacques de Molay. Ian Wilson formulated the hypothesis that the shroud had been acquired by the Templars at the sack of Constantinople in 1204, brought west by them, and given to the de Charney family for safekeeping at the time of the arrests.[10] There is no proven genealogical link between Geoffroi de Charney and the de Charney family who had the shroud in their keeping, and the Templars were not present at the sack of Constantinople, although someone who had been present could have given them the shroud. But if they had possessed such a relic surely they would have made this known, since pilgrims would have flocked to see it, and this would have increased their income.

The discovery, in the attic of a cottage in Temple Combe, Somerset, of a face painted onto a board and very similar to the face on the shroud has led to the suggestion that the Templars did indeed have the Turin Shroud at some point, and had copies made of it. However, there are many similar medieval images in existence, and no evidence to link the cottage with the Templars. A more ingenious explanation of the possible connection between the Templars' head and the shroud comes from Currer-Briggs. He suggests that the shroud was folded into a golden latticework casket with only the face showing, and this was revered by the Templars as the true image of Christ.[11]

Another theory about the head comes from Laidler, who takes the description of the head given at the trial to mean that it was an embalmed head. He speculates that it was the head of the heretical Pharoah Akenaten, and that Moses and Akenaten were the same person. The head was in the Templars' possession because they espoused an Egyptian philosophy that the perfection of knowledge could be attained, as Akenaten/Moses had attained it. The legend of the Scottish Stone of Destiny is linked to this, as being both Akenaten's throne, and the pillow on which Jacob rested. Laidler suggests that the head now rests in Rosslyn Chapel. Another author, Lynn Picknett, suggests that the embalmed head could be that of John the Baptist,[12] but if the Templars did possess an embalmed head was it not more likely that it was the head of their first Grand Master Hugues de Payens, as one brother suggested at his trial?

The legend of the Templars and the Holy Grail

The head, the grail and the Templars were related in *Perlesvaus*, and the quest for the Holy Grail has inspired authors from the middle ages onwards. In the middle ages it was the quest in itself that was important, and the grail could only be found by a perfect knight: a man without sin or blemish. He had to overcome hardships and trials of strength in order to reach the castle where the grail was kept, and then had to find his way into it. But what was the grail that he was searching for? There are many traditions surrounding the grail and what it was, some based on oral folk traditions. One tradition is that the grail was the cup used by Jesus at the Last Supper, brought to England by St Joseph of Arimathea, a convert to Christianity who had allowed Christ's body to be buried in his family tomb. Other legends maintain that he had brought the boy Jesus to Cornwall and the west of England, and this is why he later returned the grail to England. The relationship of exotic visitors and the west of England can be explained by the search for valuable minerals, tin in Cornwall and lead in the Mendip Hills of Somerset, and the ancient trade along the Atlantic coast. St Joseph of Armithea is also connected with Glastonbury in Somerset. The staff he carried was supposedly made of wood taken from the cross on which Christ was crucified. According to legend, when he placed it in the ground at Glastonbury it burst into flower and became known as the Glastonbury thorn.

An other grail story with Celtic origin suggests that St Joseph of Arithmea hid the grail containing the blood of Christ in a cupboard. Every day he lit candles before it, and prayed to it. This was noticed by the Jewish authorities and St Joseph was banished, taking with him Nicodemus who had 'carved and fashioned a head in the likeness of the Lord on the day he was on the cross'. They took the head to Jaffa and gave it to the ruler there, but they were then forced to flee again, ending up on the White Isle (Isle of Wight?). Eventually, there was a war between Joseph and his followers and the natives, and a famine followed. But Joseph prayed to God and was told to invite everyone to a feast and food would be provided, which he did, and the grail appeared at the feast.[13]

Yet another legend connects St Joseph, the grail and Mary Magdalene. Phillips suggests that St Joseph was charged to take care of Mary Magdalene by Christ, and that following the crucifixion they fled from Palestine taking with them the grail in which he had collected the holy blood as it dripped from the cross. Phillips has the couple landing in Wales, and argues that Mary Magdalene's remains and the grail were buried in Llanbabo church on Anglesey. But these were later removed by Prince Madoc of Gwynedd in 1200, before the English invaders could discover them, and hidden by him at Llanmerhymedd.[14]

The other well-known figure associated with Glastonbury is King Arthur, and it is Arthur's knights who set out to find the Holy Grail. However, the quest for the grail was probably a literary invention, written down some between 1160 and 1192 by Chrétien de Troyes, whose patron was the count of Flanders. In the prologue to *Perceval* Troyes wrote that his work was based on a book he had been given by the count, but there is no agreement as to what this book might have been.[15] The house of Flanders was connected by blood to the royal house of the kings of Jerusalem, and the counts of Flanders were inveterate crusaders. This brought a crusading element into the grail stories, and the grail quest could be seen as an analogy for a crusade. Troyes' grail epic was probably designed to be read or sung aloud at the Flanders court.[16] Troyes promoted the cycle of Arthurian legends in the high middle ages, and the quest for the grail and Arthur's knights, Lancelot, Tristram, Perceval and Gawain became inextricably mixed with the grail stories in the medieval mind.

Arthur may have been a real person, a British leader fighting to retain Roman civilization against the pagan barbarian Saxons, but most of what we know about him comes from romance, where his knights wear armour and carry the banners of the medieval knight rather than the Dark Age war leader. How did the Knights Templar, who *were* a real group of men, become associated with the fictional Arthurian legends? It came about through another fictional work, *Parzival* by Wolfram von Eschenbach, written between 1182 and 1188. In *Parzival* the guardian of the grail castle is called *Templeis.*[17] This has been taken to mean Templar or templar with a lower-case 't', meaning someone who lived in a temple. However, in German, the language of von Eschenbach, the Knights Templar were known as *templeherren*. The suffix *eise* could mean protector, or in Dutch, which is close to medieval German, the word *eiser* means prosecutor or plaintiff – one who asks questions, and the grail questors in *Parzival* had to answer a number of questions before they could reach the inner sanctum where the grail was kept. The idea of questions that have to be answered correctly before the grail can be accessed also appears in Celtic stories attached to the grail where a country that is under a spell can only be released by answering correctly and gaining the grail.

Von Eschenbach's *Templeisen* prowl the grounds of the grail castle to repel intruders. They are chaste, but their badge is not a red cross as the Templars wore, but a turtle dove, the symbol of love and peace. Perhaps it is natural that the juxtaposition of the knights of the Temple of Solomon and the keepers of the temple of the grail occurred, although it has to be remembered that the medieval grail romances are fiction. By the nineteenth century, however, it was thought that von Eschenback might have woven truth into his fictional story, and it came to be believed that the Knights Templar really were the guardians of the grail; and by the twentieth century it was even suggested that von Eschenbach had modelled his grail stories on the Knights Templar.

The grail itself could have been a chalice used to collect Christ's blood,[18] or a shallow silver dish or *graal*. However, there is a far-fetched but interesting theory, exploited in speculative and popular writings, that the words *san greal* should be written *sang real* or blood royal. The blood royal in question is supposed to be the continuation of the Christ's line through progeny of Christ and Mary Magdalene.

Mary Magdalene and the Templars

It has been suggested that the Knights Templar held a weighty secret that would destroy Christianity and the Catholic Church: that Christ had not been the Son of God but the Son of Joseph, and as a man had sexual inter-course with Mary Magdalene from which a child was born; this child bore the royal blood of Christ and Mary in his or her veins, and that this blood-line continued through the ages.[19] Medieval legends show how Mary Magdalene and the Knights Templar could be interwoven, but first we need to ask who was the Biblical Mary Magdalene? The name Magdalene is assumed to come from Magdala, and the claim is made that she was of the royal lineage of the house of Benjamin, and thus Christ's social equal. But which of the New Testament Marys is she? Is she the same Mary who listened to Christ, whilst her sister Martha toiled away at the housework, and whose brother Lazarus was raised from the dead by Christ? Later legends suggest that this was the most likely Mary, but was this the same Mary who smashed an alabaster jar of ointment over Christ's feet and dried them with her hair? She could be the woman who was going to be stoned for adultery who was rescued by Christ, or she could have been a prostitute who found redemption for her sins through Christ's teaching. The idea that Mary Magdalene was a fallen woman can be traced to the Golden Legend of 1267, which says that Mary Magdalene was born of noble parents, the descendants of kings. But she forsook her heritage and became a common sinner, who found salvation through Christ.[20]

Mary Magdalene's most important role in the Christian faith was being the first person to meet the risen Christ, either as one of the three Marys who had gone to the tomb, or alone. She may also have been pre-sent at Pentecost when the disciples received the gift of tongues, so that they could go out into the world and spread the Christian message. In some legends she becomes a missionary and this connects her to France. The story goes that some time after the Ascension of Christ, unbelievers set Mary Magdalene, her sister Martha and brother Lazarus, St Maximin, and a girl servant adrift in a rudderless boat. They eventually drifted ashore at Marseilles, and took shelter in the portico of a pagan temple. As people came to sacrifice to the pagan gods, Mary was seized with the desire to convert them to Christianity, and began to preach to them. She converted the prince of the land and his people, and then south-western France was divided into provinces, with Mary taking Aix as her portion, and Lazarus becoming the first bishop of Marseilles.

The Golden Legend claims that Mary withdrew to a cave for 30 years; other legends place her in a cave directly after the Ascension, and state that during the time she was in a cave, the desert land burst into flower and became a paradise of delights. There are echoes here of the belief expressed by one Templar at the French trial that the Templar idol could make the waste land to flower.

A further similarity between evidence given by the Templars at their trial and the legend of Mary Magdalene comes from another story told about her. After she had converted the prince of Marseilles, he wanted evidence of what she had told him from St Peter himself who was in Rome. He set off to Rome by sea, taking his wife, who had become pregnant by a miracle, with him. A great storm blew up during the voyage, and the wife went into labour. She died but the baby survived. The sailors wanted to cast them both into the sea, but the prince persuaded them to leave mother and baby on a flat rock. This was done and he continued to Rome. On his way back he found that through Mary Magdalene's intercession both mother and baby were alive. The mother told him that whilst he was in Rome, she had gone there with Mary Magdalene and had witnessed his meeting with St Peter.

How does the continuation of Christ's blood-line through Mary Magdalene fit with the Templar legend? A legend persisted in the East that Mary had lived with Jesus and the disciples for 11 years after the resurrection, and that Mary was one of Christ's inner-circle.[21] A legend from the early Greek Church taught that after the Resurrection Mary went to Ephesus with St John the Divine, and converted the heathen there. But Honorius of Auton suggested that after the crucifixion she went instead to Rome to accuse Pontius Pilate of condemning an innocent man. Whilst in Rome, according to the Gospel of Nicodemus, she met the physician Galen who could make the blind see. However, Galen lived a century after Christ.[22] The addition to the legend of a marriage or at least a sexual relationship between Jesus and Mary Magdalene comes from inferences drawn from the gospel of St Philip, which is dated to about AD 400. The writer of the gospel makes it clear that he is not Philip the Apostle who had been charged with recording the sayings of Christ, but implies that his gospel is a copy of those sayings. A copy of it was one of the Gnostic codices found at Nag Hammadi in 1947. Coptic scholars do indeed suggest that the gospel is a copy of an earlier text.[23]

The gospel of Philip was not included in the New Testament scriptures and cannot be seen as a primary source on the life and sayings of

Jesus. Furthermore, there is some doubt about the translation of some of the words in it, and also the editorial interpolations of words missing from the scroll, which has made the whole open to misinterpretation. The crucial passages on Christ and Mary read: 'We receive conception from grace which is among us. There were three who walked with the Lord at all times. Mary his mother and her sister, and Magdalene whom they call his consort.'[24] Some interpretations suggest that the interpretation should be her consort, meaning the friend of Mary mother of Jesus, rather than the consort or partner of Jesus himself.

Further on in the gospel we learn that 'The Lord loved Mary more than all other disciples and kissed her on the [mouth] often.'[25] The document is damaged at the word after 'the', and 'mouth' is a translator's interpolation. The kiss could have been on her forehead, cheek, hand or elsewhere. The others said to him, 'Why do you love her more than all of us?' The Saviour answered to them, 'Why do I not love you like her?' This is followed by a metaphor of a blind man getting his sight back, symbolizing the salvation of the sinner coming from darkness into light.[26] This may have similarities to theories about the symbolism of the Templars' black-and-white banner, representing the triumph of good/white over evil/black.

The gospel continues with a treatise about the benefits of marriage between good people, and its essential element in carrying on the line and the word, 'man and wife are image and angel united.'[27] In fact much of the gospel is a Gnostic marriage-guidance tract, and it is not surprising that commentators have seen it as evidence of a marriage between Jesus and Mary, and the kiss as evidence of a sexual liaison. However, the Gnostics thought that the secret of knowledge was conveyed by a kiss, and in kissing Mary, Jesus was passing on his knowledge to her. This is what the jealous disciples objected to, as it set Mary up as their equal in knowledge, and of course as we have seen in some legends she becomes an apostle and a missionary, converting the south of France to Christianity.

Here was something the Catholic Church really could object to, as it ran counter to the role of women as laid down by Church,[28] that women could not intercede between Man and God, or give the sacrament. If the Templars held a secret that showed Mary acting as an apostle and a priest, then they did indeed hold a dangerous and heretical secret which would make the Templars the allies of the Cathars and Albigensians who allowed women to preach and give the sacrament.

Modern authors dealing with the Mary Magdalene legend are more concerned with the marriage of Christ and Mary. One mediaeval legend suggested that she married St John the Evangelist rather than Christ, and another that she was pregnant when rescued by Christ from stoning by the mob for adultery. In the fourteenth century Jacques de Vitry wrote: 'when Christ contracted marriage with this sinner, she gave birth to many souls as she had converted many to penance by her example.'[29] Mary here is an allegorical figure or the Church, and throughout the legends we are looking at a spiritual rather than a physical motherhood, although some mediaeval legends expressed Mary Magdalene's sexuality in such terms as 'Mary hungered in spirit for the Word of God, which in a wonderful manner excited her desire again and again. Drawn by the sweetness of her beloved, she became drunk on the heavenly cup of desire, composing herself and raising herself up, so that she dissolved at last in the heat of a most chaste love, she drank in interior joy.'[30]

The diverse elements of the grail story, and the idea that Mary Magdalene and Jesus had a child, attracted the attention of a French journalist, Gerard de Sede, who was a member of a surrealist group of French artists and writers, including the a fantastist Pierre Plantard de St Claire, who thought he was descended from the French Merovingian kings, and a nobleman, Philippe de Cherisy, who had a taste for adventure and the bizarre. Together they amassed evidence that Plantard was indeed heir to the French throne and could trace his lineage back to Dagobert II. They constructed an organization called the Priory of Sion, and endowed it with a mythical series of illustrious grand priors, who included Leonardo da Vinci and Sir Isaac Newton. They wrote coded documents outlining this, and claimed that they had found these hidden in a broken pillar in the church of Rennes le Chateau in south-west France. In the nineteenth century, apparently, the parish priest of Rennes le Chateau had left for Paris and returned suddenly and inexplicably rich. The trio made up a story that he too had found documents in the church that proved something so terrible that the Catholic Church had paid him a vast sum to keep quiet. The encoded documents were eventually deposited in the Bibliothèque Nationale in France, in what became known as *Le dossier secret*. The whole thing had started as a hoax but soon got out of hand. The documents were 'decoded' and the theory developed that the priest had been paid off because he had found evidence of the marriage of Jesus Christ and Mary Magdalene, and the continuation of their blood line through the Merovingian kings. When *The Holy Blood and the Holy Grail* was first published in 1976, Monsieur Plantard found to his amazement that he was being being portrayed as the descendant of Christ, something he was quick to deny.

Two theories implicate the Templars in this saga. One says that the Templars found evidence of the marriage of Mary Magdalene and Christ in the Temple of Solomon and brought this to France with them. At the time of their arrests this was taken out of the country and hidden, eventually ending up in the priory of Sion. The other theory is that before the Templars received the evidence it was in the hands of the heretical Cathars. Shortly before the fall of the Cathar fortress at Montsegur to the Catholics, the evidence was secretly taken away and given to the Knights Templar for safekeeping until it was claimed by the priory of Sion. There are also geographical links between the Templars and Mary Magdalene in France. Two churches claimed to have her relics: Vezelay in Burgundy and St Maximin, 20 miles north-east of Marseilles. Both were in prime Templar territory. The Dominicans of St Maximin had the better claim as all the legends about Mary in France placed her in that area. But Vezelay had a royal patron, Louis IX the crusader king. Vezelay claimed to have acquired their relics by divine providence. These were kept in a bronze reliquary, which was opened in 1265 to reveal bones wrapped in silk.[31] The alleged role of the Knights Templar with the bloodline of Christ is only one of the many theories that surround the Order, and their fabled, if it exists, treasure has yet to be found.

The Knights Templar and the treasure-hunters

Templar treasure-hunters fall into two categories: those who hope to find mystical treasure and those who hope to find the real wealth of the Templars. Gold and jewels were seen going into the London and Paris Temples, but were not on the inventories taken in 1307 and 1308, as we have seen, so what happened to these, and might these riches still be hidden somewhere?[32]

The first question to be asked is whether it was material treasure that the priest François Saunière found at Rennes le Chateau in the nineteenth century? After his return from Paris with his unexplained wealth he did not stop searching. He was seen digging in the parish graveyard at night, and gathering stacks of stones from various places. When he died his housekeeper was seen burning stacks of banknotes, and when asked about these, is said to have told the inquirers to look around them if they sought treasure, leading to the belief that something was still hidden in the area.[33]

One theory located the key to finding the treasure in a seventeenth-century painting by Poussin depicting shepherds around a tomb, set in a landscape similar to that in the vicinity of Rennes le Chateau. On the tomb is inscribed *Et in Arcadia ego* (I too was in Arcadia).[34] The painting is now in the Louvre.

Code-Masters Blake and Blezard took a copy of the picture and constructed a pentagram over it, and then applied the five points of the pentagram to the landscape, marking where the points come to rest, and using other geometric calculations built up a network of lines and points, which might reveal where the treasure was hidden.[35]

Henry Lincoln also used the Poussin painting as a key to decoding the Rennes le Chateau mystery. He too identified the landscape in the painting as being that around Rennes le Chateau, but when he contacted the art expert Anthony Blunt about this he was told that it was mere coincidence, and there was no evidence that Poussin had ever visited that part of France.[36] Undeterred, Lincoln continued on his quest, and using a pentagonal system of geometry built up a network of alignments that he suggests form a gigantic Temple. But who built this, when, why or how, he does not know.[37] Lincoln's geometry was re-worked by Richard Andrews and Paul Schellenberg. Their conclusions involved the Knights Templar directly in the Rennes le Chateau mystery. They argue that the Knights Templar retrieved the body of Christ from Jerusalem, had it embalmed and took it to France where they buried it on the Lampos rock formation on Mont Cardou.[38]

So far a large number of lines have bisected the landscape, but no treasure has been found. Could it have been taken to Scotland in October 1307? This theory suggests that some Templars escaped from France using their fleet anchored at La Rochelle. They sailed round the coast of

Ireland, making landfall on the Isle of Mull, and settling at a place called Kilmartin in Argyll.[39] The Kilmartin area in Scotland is stuffed full of antiquities, ranging from prehistoric times to the seventeenth century. There are chamber tombs, cup-and-ring stones, henges, and engraved grave markers showing swords and knights in armour. The gravestones are thought to represent Templar knights who died in the area, although there is no evidence of the Templars ever coming to rest there. However, the Templar treasure was thought not to be hidden at Kilmartin, but to have been moved elsewhere.

If the Templar treasure actually existed and is still hidden somewhere, it may be that the treasure-hunters are looking in the wrong place. For example is it on the Danish island of Bornholm, which possesses a remarkable number of churches, and an unusual number of finds of gold plaques showing a longhaired man? Haagenson and Lincoln have used geometry to suggest that the island was linked to the Templars and their treasure.[40] Although there is no evidence that the Templars carried away their treasure from France on board ship, there is evidence of them disposing of property in Aragon. Here there was resistance to the arrests, and the Templar castles were fortified. The Templars had a month's warning to make preparations, and rather than let their possessions fall into the hands of the inquisitors, some were sold off, relics, jewels and money was given to the Knights Hospitaller, and other property was concealed.[41] The treasure could, it is postulated, have been taken over an escape route in the Pyrenees and into Spain, but need it have remained in Europe? It could have been smuggled out via the Rock of Gibralter to Morocco, or even hidden on the rock itself.

The truth of the matter is however that, there was and is no treasure to be found. The gold, silver and jewels seen going into the London and Paris Temples did not belong to the Knights Templar. They were keeping it safe for others as part of their role as safe-deposit bankers, and the legend of the Templars' treasure is just that – a legend.

The legend of the Templars and the Freemasons

There is one more legacy that the Knights Templar are reputed to have left to us today – the Freemasons. To look at the origins of that body we have to jump forward four centuries from the death of Jacques de Molay to the eighteenth century. During this century great social change was taking place across Europe. Three elements of this change are relevant here. One was the growth of the middle classes, educated and articulate people who took a lively interest in the unknown; the second was the proliferation of print, newspapers, journals and pamphlets which encouraged debates on larger issues than the local community; and the third was the need for places where these debates could take place, outside the private space of the home or the public forum of the Stock Exchange, or the houses of parliament or national assembly. Coffee houses fulfilled this need. These were places where men could meet, read the newspapers, and discuss the affairs of the day. Certain coffee houses is England became known for certain political alliances, and from there it was but a step to closing the doors to outsiders, and founding a club with a discreet or even secret membership.

The eighteenth century was the age of clubs, and no club was more influential and long lasting than the Freemasons. The Grand Lodge of Britain was formed in 1717, and by 1768 there were 300 affiliated lodges.[42] The masons developed secret signs, and insignia based on the Temple of Solomon as described in the Biblical book of Ezekiel, which was one link to the Templars, but there were soon a number of splinter groups, all of whom sought to prove the antiquity of their particular brand of masonry. It was an exiled Jacobite Scot, Andrew Ramsey, who made the connection between the masons and the crusaders, suggesting that the masons had crusading origins, and although he did not actually mention the Templars he hinted at it, and it was left to a German branch of the masons to claim an actual link between the last Templar Grand Master and the first Masonic Templar Grand Master. This link was proved to their satisfaction in 1804 when a charter was discovered in France which showed an unbroken line of Grand Masters from Jacques de Molay who handed over his office to John Larmenius. The Larmenius charter, as it became known, is an obvious forgery, but despite its shortcomings it was accepted as evidence of the antiquity of the Templar masons, and their origin in the Knights Templar.[43]

The continental masons were not the only lodge of Templar masons. Another group existed in Scotland who claimed that they too were descended from Knights Templar who had fled from France and settled in Scotland. Here, it is claimed, they joined craft guilds, and their gravestones can be identified in Scottish churchyards by the symbols of their trades engraved on them.[44]

One member of the Templar masons was an English admiral, William Sydney Smith, who settled in Paris. In a book dedicated to him and published in 1840, James Burnes shows how nineteenth-century members interpreted the medieval vows of poverty and obedience. Poverty was interpreted as a readiness to help and share with other members, and obedience meant obedience to the State and the Grand Master of the Order.[45] What they thought about the row of chastity is not stated.

England has a claim to be the place where the link between the Knights Templar and the masons took place. John Robinson suggests that a group of Templars, having learnt about the arrests in France, went into hiding in Essex to avoid arrest. They reorganized themselves to emerge as a secret society, and were instrumental in organizing the network that spread rebellion across the south and east of England at the time of the Peasant's Revolt.[46] There is some logic in this. The Templars did have important property in Essex and Hertfordshire, the counties at the heart of the revolt, and one of the peasants' leaders, Wat Tyler, had what could be construed as masonic links. But in that case where had the Templars been in the 73 years between the arrests and the revolt?

The Freemasons and the Knights Templar have one more blow to inflict upon history. Levi suggests that prior to the French Revolution there was a 'silent conspiracy' which vowed to destroy the 'social edifice' which had sentenced Jacques de Molay. The conspirators met in the house of Jean-Jacques Rousseau, who was allegedly a mason. This became the centre of revolutionary activity, in which the scaffold on which the French king was to die formed a central part of the revenge brought by the masons for Jacques de Molay's death.[47]

Finally, we return to Scotland. Baigent and Leigh argue that the Templars were the conduit through which Freemasonry in Scotland passed into the seventeenth century. They suggest that the Scottish Grand Lodge owed much to a Templar heritage, and it was from Scotland that the craft spread into France and the New World.[48] Freemasonry links the Knights Templar, the Sinclair family and the eerily mysterious Rosslyn Chapel in the village of Roslin near Edinburgh. The Sinclairs were the hereditary patrons of masonry in chapels, and they built this chapel, which has imagery in it that could be masonic.

All roads lead to Rosslyn Chapel

The village of Roslin is seven miles from Edinburgh. The chapel was founded in 1446 by Sir William Sinclair and was to be the private place of worship for him and his family when they were at Roslin Castle. It was also to be his family mausoleum, and to facilitate the Sinclair souls' entry into heaven he made it a collegiate foundation dedicated to St Matthew with a college of priests to sing perpetual masses for the Sinclairs. The original plan was cruciform, but the founder died before it could be completed, so it is box-shaped, a typical Perpendicular building with flying buttresses. Inside it is a mass of carvings, which have been interpreted in many ways. They could be of masonic origin and are part of the cement that links the masons and the Knights Templar. There is a family link as a William Sinclair was the first Scottish Grand Master of the masons. James Green, author of a book about Rosslyn Chapel, suggests that Robert the Bruce created Freemasonry after the Battle of Bannockburn as a way to protect and hide the Knights Templar who had helped him to win the battle.[49] There is also a link between the Bruce and the Sinclairs, as it was a Sir William Sinclair who was charged with taking the Bruce's heart to be buried in Jerusalem, but died on the journey. Green also sees a link between America, Rosslyn and the Knights Templar, identifying the decoration of an arch in the chapel as Indian corn and suggesting that the Templars funded Henry Sinclair to take a voyage of exploration in the fourteenth century, during which he discovered America. Green also identifies a cactus amongst carvings by the south door.[50]

The Templar connection with Rosslyn Chapel is further explored by Sabina Ross Strachan who suggests that Sir William Sinclair's tombstone shows him to be a high-ranking Templar, 'a grand prior in fact', because the tomb is the appropriate size for the burial of a skull and leg bones, 'in a style reminiscent of known Templar burials.'[51] However, there are no known Templar burial customs, and this was the Sir William who died taking the Bruce's heart to Jerusalem. The flesh would have been boiled from the bones in order to return these for burial in Scotland.

Those looking for masonic elements at Rosslyn have homed in on 'the Apprentice Pillar', and the legend attached to it that a master mason was shown a drawing of a similar column in Rome, and left to study it. Whilst he was away his apprentice completed the column, and when he returned the master mason was so angry he killed the apprentice. This has similarities with the story of Hiram Abif and the building of Solomon's temple, which is part of masonic lore. Similar stories surround other works of art in religious buildings, and the carving could in fact be the work of the Derbyshire Prentice family of stone-carvers, who are known to have been working in Scotland at the time Rosslyn Chapel was built.

Geometric analysis of the chapel has also produced theories that link it to some great secret, perhaps the hiding-place of the Holy Grail. The hollow at the base of the Apprentice Pillar has been X-rayed, and produced nothing, but the main focus for a search for the grail is the crypt behind the choir. The vaults under the nave are said to house the tombs of the Sinclair family, including knights in full armour.[52] There is no evidence for the latter, and the idea probably comes from Sir Walter Scott's *Ballad of Rosabelle*, which describes how when a member of the Sinclair family nears death, the chapel is lit by unearthly flames. The poem says:

> *Roslin's chiefs uncoffined lie*
> *Each baron for a sabled shroud*
> *Sheathed in his iron panoply . . .*[53]

Rosslyn Chapel can lend itself to any theory, and will continue to fascinate those who like mysteries and conspiracies.

Notes

1 K. Jolly, C. Raudvere, E. Peters, *Witchcraft and Magic in Europe. The Middle Ages*, London: Athlone Press (2002), p. 219.

2 Noel Currer-Briggs suggests that Yalla = Selah, the Saracen battle cry. N. Currer-Briggs, *The Holy Grail and the Shroud of Christ*, Maulden, Bedfordshire: ARA Publications (1984), 94: see also L. Picknett, *Mary Magdalene Christianity's Hidden Goddess*, London: Robinson (2003), p. 104.

3 See for example the website www.general-anaesthesia/com/image/ mandgragora/html, last consulted 18 May 2006.

4 M. Barber, *The New Knighthood*, Cambridge: CUP (1995), p. 1.

5 R. Loomis, *The Grail from Celtic Myth to Christian Symbol*, Cardiff: University of Wales Press (1963), pp. 55–6, 103.

6 E. Lord, *The Knights Templar in Britain*, London: Pearson Education (2004), p. 281.

7 M. Lambert, *Medieval Heresy*, Oxford: Blackwell (3rd ed. 2005), 62–3.

8 Lambert, p. 195.

9 Lambert, p. 38.

10 I. Wilson, *The Turin Shroud*, Harmondsworth Penguin (1979); M. Barber, 'The Turin Shroud' in Barber, M. *Crusaders and heretics from the 12th to the 14th centuries*, Aldershot: Variorum VI (1995); I. Wilson, *The Blood and the Shroud*, London: Weidenfeld and Nicolson (1998).

11 Currer-Briggs, p. 192.

12 K. Laidler, *The Head of God*, London: Weidenfeld and Nicolson (1998), pp. 4, 6, 42; Picknett, p. 102.

13 Loomis, pp. 46–64, 223, 226–7.

14 G. Phillips, *The Marian Conspiracy*, London: Sidgwick and Jackson (2000), p. 309.

15 J. Goering, *The Virgin and the Grail. Origins of a Legend*, London: Yale University Press (2005), p. 11.

16 A. Divenes, 'The grail and the Third Crusade: Thoughts on Le Conte de Grael by Chrétien de Troyes, *Arthurian Literature*, X (1990), pp. 13–109.

17 Goering has *templeise*, which is singular, one of a company of knights who guard the grail. Richard Barber has *templeisen*, plural. R. Barber, *The Holy Grail*, London: Allen and Unwin (2004), p. 308.

18 Barber, p. 48.

19 This is the main argument of M. Baigent, R. Leigh and H. Lincoln, *The Holy Blood and the Holy Grail* London: Arrow Books (1982) and the plot of D. Brown, *The Da Vinci Code*, London: Corgi (2004).

20 A translation of the Golden Legend can be found in D. McCoff, *The Life of St Mary Magdalene and of her sister Martha*, Kalamazoo: Cistercian Publications (1989).

21 H.M. Garth, *Saint Mary Magdalene in Medieval Literature*, Baltimore: Johns Hopkins University Press (1950), p. 71.

22 Garth, pp. 40–3.

23 J. Filson, *A New Testament History*, London: SCM (1964), p. 304.

24 The translation used here is R. McK Wilson, *The Gospel of Philip*, London: A.R. Mowbray (1962), pp. 35, 97. Wilson translates the word between 'call' and 'consort' as 'his' but points out that an earlier translator H. Schenke translated it as 'her'.

25 Wilson, p. 39.

26 Wilson, p. 41.

27 Wilson, p. 35.

28 St Paul's first letter to Timothy, chapter 2, verses 11–12.

29 K. Janson, *The Making of the Magdalene*, Princeton Princeton University Press (1999), pp. 25, 242.

30 McCoff, p. 95.

31 R. Clements, 'The Cult of Mary Magdalene in late medieval France', in T. Head (ed.), *Medieval Hagiography*, London: Garland Publishing (2000), p. 657.

32 If the English Templars hid any treasure then Temple Ewell in Kent is the place to look, as this was where many of the Templar officers from the London Temple were arrested, perhaps on their way to escape by sea from Dover.

33 Picknett, pp. 108, 110.

34 The key book on Poussin is by Anthony Blunt.

35 P. Blake, and P.S. Blezard *The Arcadian Cipher*, London: Sidgwick and Jackson (2000), p. 33.

36 H. Lincoln, *The Holy Place*, London: Jonathan Cape (1991), p. 58.

37 Lincoln, pp. 104, 122.

38 R. Andrews, and P. Schellenberg, *The Tomb of God*, London: Little, Brown (2000), pp. 69, 286, 381, 395, 423.

39 M. Baigent and R. Leigh *The Temple and the Lodge*, London: Arrow Books (1989), pp. 24–35, 102–10.

40 E. Haagenson and H. Lincoln, *The Templars' Secret Island. The Knight, the Priest and the Treasure*, London: Windrush Press (2000). Their reasoning is that a nineteenth-century illustration shows Templars with long hair; these are Norman-style churches on Bornholm; and Estil, archbishop of Lund, was a friend of St Bernard of Clairvaux. pp. 5, 26, 32–3.

41 A. Forey, *The Fall of the Templars in the Corona of Aragon*, Aldershot: Ashgate (2001), p. 14.

42 R. Porter, (2000) *Enlightenment*, Harmondsworth: Penguin, Books, p. 38. In latter years the masons have become much more open, and it is possible to tour some of their lodges. The author would like to thank Dr Paul Richards for arranging a visit to the remarkable eighteenth-century lodge, enclosed within the heart of a hotel in Kings Lynn.

43 Lord, pp. 277–8.

44 Scottish gravestones often have the insignia of the person's trade upon them, such as an anvil for a blacksmith, a hammer, or a trowel. This does not mean that these are Templar graves.

45 J. Burnes, *Sketches of the History of the Knights Templar*, Edinburgh (1844), pp. 48, 51.

46 J. Robinson, *Born in Blood. The Last Secrets of Freemasonry*, London: Century Books (1989), p. xix.

47 Baigent and Leigh, pp. 61–9, 110–15, 190–1, 207, 235, 247, 298–336.

48 E. Levi, *The History of Magic*, London: William Rider and Son (2nd ed. 1922), 265–6.

49 J. Green, *Rosslyn Chapel. The Enigma and the Myth*, Fort William: Templar Arch Publications (2002), pp. 4, 19.

50 Green, pp. 3–4.

51 S. Strachan, *The Mystery of Rosslyn Chapel Exhibition Catalogue*, self-published (1996), p. 15.

52 Green, p. 3.

53 Quoted in G.W. Wilson, *Photographs of Scottish Scenery: Edinburgh and Roslin*, Edinburgh: William Ritchie (1892), np.

Conclusion

At the start of this book we saw Jacques de Molay facing his death at the stake. He was the representative of a proud order of knights who had fought and died for Christendom, and had been the advisers and friends of kings. They had been brought down by a French king who needed cash and had ambitious political and religious motives and the great advantage of a pope whose actions he could control. They had also been brought down by their pride and the secrecy with which they conducted their affairs. The chronicler put a curse into Jacques de Molay's mouth as he stood before the pyre. Was this curse put to rest by the deaths of the French pope and the French king who condemned the Order, or are the many theories, legends and ideas about the Templars part of our inheritance of the Templar's curse?

The Templar legend is extremely durable and each age invents its own version of the Knights Templar. Let us close with a good example of this, a poem by W.B. Yeats which relates the fate of Jacques de Molay to Ireland at the time of the Civil War of 1919.

> I climb to the tower-top and lean upon broken stone,
> A mist that is like blown snow is sweeping over all,
> Valley, river, and elms, under the light of a moon
> That seems unlike itself, that seems unchangeable,
> A glittering sword out of the east. A puff of wind
> And those white glimmering fragments of the mist sweep by.
> Frenzies bewilder, reveries perturb the mind;
> Monstrous familiar images swim to the mind's eye.
>
> Vengeance upon the murderers,' the cry goes up,
> Vengeance for Jacques de Molay'. In cloud-pale rags or in lace,
> The rage-driven, rage-tormented, and rage-hungry troop,
> Trooper belabouring trooper, biting at arm or at face

Plunges towards nothing, arms and fingers spreading wide
For the embrace of nothing; and I, my wits astray
Because of all that senseless tumult, all but cried
For vengeance on the murderers of Jacques Molay.

W.B. Yeats, *Meditations in the Time of Civil War*, VII (1919)

Glossary

absolution forgiveness for sins committed against God, pronounced by a priest

advowson right to present someone to a vacant ecclesiastical benefice

Albigensians alternative name for the Cathars (q.v.)

apostate someone who has abandoned their faith or religious commitment

Benedictines monks or nuns following the Rule of St Benedict

book of hours book containing details of the religious services for each part of the day

boon work extra work demanded on top of labour services at special times e.g. harvest

bordar unfree smallholder; sometimes an alternative name for a cottar

canon law the law of the Church

caravan group of merchants or other travellers and their pack animals, travelling in the desert

Cathars heretical group flourishing in the eleventh and twelfth centuries, whose beliefs included reincarnation and dualist doctrines, and rejected the priesthood

chain mail linked circles of iron forming a protective singlet or shirt, worn over a leather jerkin or tunic

chamber tomb room-like tomb of someone of high status, often containing grave goods to accompany the dead person to the next life

chapter meeting meeting of monks or canons to discuss matters relating to their own monastery or cathedral

charter document confirming privileges or asset-transfer; e.g. town charters often conferred borough status or confirmed the right to hold a fair

commandery unit of Templar government, focusing on a local group of Templars under the charge of a commander

consecrated host the bread after the prayer of consecration, in Catholic doctrine the moment when the bread becomes the body of Christ

consistory court ecclesiastical court, usually presided over by a bishop, dealing with any matters relevant to the Church and its concerns

corrodian lay person (often elderly) who paid a sum of money to a monastery or other religious house in return for long-term lodging and food

cottar unfree smallholder, usually farming on subsistence level or below, and therefore available to do paid work in addition to the labour-service obligations owed to his lord

crusader state state created after the conquest by crusaders of a formerly Muslim-held area in the Middle East

dalmatic a priest's liturgical outer robe, usually in the form of a long, wide-sleeved tunic

Dominicans religious order of friars (travelling preachers) founded by St Dominic in the early thirteenth century; concentrated on intellectual matters and were put in charge of the Inquisition

dualism influential religious doctrine of good and evil eternally in opposition to each other

esquire junior knight responsible for serving and accompanying a knight who has already been dubbed and spurred

excommunicate shut out from all religious services, especially the mass, thus removing the possibility of absolution

feudalism system of society relating landholding to service obligations; high-status lords (magnates) held directly from the king and owed him military service; unfree peasants (serfs) held from magnates or lower-status lords and owed them labour services

feudal law law governing the social system in a feudal society

feudal society society whose social bonds were formed by feudalism

fief parcel of land or estate held in return for military service

Franciscans order of friars (travelling preachers) founded by St Francis of Assisi in the early thirteenth century; concentrated on living simply and caring for the poor

freeman peasant holding his land without labour service obligations

galley sea-going ship with oars

Gnostic sect quasi-heretical Christian group relying on special religious experience and myth rather than following Catholic doctrine or Biblical revelation

heresy belief that departs from orthodox dogma

heriot fee or 'fine' payable to the lord by an unfree tenant when entering a new holding, often on the death of the previous tenant

in camera in private

interdict ban proclaimed by the Church, usually associated with excommunication

Inquisition wing of the Church devoted to maintaining the purity of Catholic belief

Knights Hospitaller Order of St John of Jerusalem, religious order founded in 1119 initially to care for sick and impoverished pilgrims to the Holy Land; later the Order became involved with the defence of pilgrims and developed a military wing

labour service work on the land owed by unfree peasants to their landlord as a condition of their landholding

linguistic province unit of Templar government based on contemporary regions, e.g. the English province

mangonel siege-engine used to catapult missiles in an attempt to breach castle walls

manorial court court presided over by the lord of a manor or estate, which settled disputes between tenants and oversaw land transfers and other legal documents

memorial effigy statue, often in stone or metal, depicting a dead person as he or she was when alive

missal book of prayers said as part of the mass

obit roll list of gifts to a church or religious institution, with the day of the donor's death when he or she is to have special prayers

papal bull proclamation made by the pope on a specific subject

paternoster Latin version of the Lord's Prayer, beginning 'Pater Noster'

penance actions performed by a penitent to show their contrition; for a medieval Catholic these might include a pilgrimage, charitable giving or the saying of special prayers

perdition loss of the hope of heaven; eternal damnation or consignment to hell

Perpendicular style of ecclesiastical architecture developed in the late fourteenth and early fifteenth century, characterized by big windows with horizontal bars and ornate roof construction

pilgrimage religious journey taken by the pious or the penitent to a holy place or shrine

Poor Clares Franciscan group of nuns devoted to contemplative and intercessory prayer

prelate senior churchman, e.g. bishop or archbishop

preceptor local monastic official or administrator of a regional headquarters

Purgatory journey towards the perfection required for entry into Paradise, taken after death; often seen as a place of torment or struggle, from which the dead person could be released or relieved by the prayers of the living

racked tortured on the rack; this involved fastening the prisoner's ankles and wrists to the corners of the instrument and then bending or stretching the body

relic something belonging to a holy person, often some of their bones, kept by religious groups or individuals in the belief that they will help the possessor

religious foundation organized religious group, e.g. a monastery or religious order

religious guild lay group of people linked by religious belief or purpose, which functioned as a medieval charity

reliquary box or other receptacle for a holy relic

rent in kind rent paid in goods rather than money

serf unfree feudal peasant, including bordars, cottars and villeins

siege engine machine used to breach or climb walls, including mangonels, siege towers and battering rams

siege tower tower built, usually of wood, in an attempt to scale the walls of a castle of town under siege

simony corrupt practice whereby ecclesiastical posts or benefices were allotted by favouritism or as a result of payment rather than by merit

sortie attack on besiegers by the besieged, usually as part of a strategy to end a siege

sub-infeudated provided a subcontracted fief with military service owed to a magnate rather than directly to the king

Teutonic knight German order of religious/crusading knights formed in the late twelfth century

the sacrament the consecrated host taken during the mass

tithes ecclesiastical taxes, traditionally a tenth of a person's income

troubadour musicians and singer-songwriters retelling the stories of chivalrous adventures of mythical knights and kings

turcopolier Templar military leader, between the rank of sergeant and knight

undermine method of tunnelling or digging under castle walls so as to cause their collapse, a military engineering tactic used in sieges

villein unfree peasant, usually prosperous and holding an amount of land sufficient to feed a family

Bibliography

Place of publication is London unless otherwise mentioned.

Primary Sources

Brand, G.J. (ed. & trans.), *Roll of Arms of Edward I (1272–1307)*, Woodbridge: The Boydell Press (1997)

Burton, Thomas de, *Chronica Monasterii de Melsa*, HMSO (1967 repr)

Calendar of Close Rolls 1307–1313, HMSO (1908)

Calendar of Inquisitions Post-Mortem, Vol. 1, HMSO (1904)

Calendar of Patent Rolls, ed. T. Hardy, HMSO (1903)

Clairvaux, St Bernard of, *In Praise of the New Knighthood*, trans. Conrad Greenia, Cistercian Fathers Series, Cistercian Publications (1977)

D'Albon, Marquis, *Cartulaire Generale de l'Ordre du Templiers*, Paris: Librairie Ancienne Honoré Champion (1913)

De Deuil, Odo, *De Perfectione Ludovic VII in Orientem*, New York: Records of Civilization Sources and Studies VII (1948)

Finke, H., *Pappstum und Untergang des Templeorden*, Munster: Druck und Verlag der Aschendorffeschen Buchhandlung (1907)

Fowler, J.T., *Cistercian Statutes AD 1256–7*, Bradbury and Co (1890)

Fraser, C.M., *Records of Anthony Bek, 1283–1311*, Surtees Society (1953)

Gabrielli, F. (trans.), *Arab Historians of the Crusades*, Routledge (1984)

Garmonsway, G. (ed.), *The Anglo-Saxon Chronicle*, Dent (1986)

Gerald of Wales, *The Journey Through Wales/The Description of Wales*, ed. and trans. L. Thorpe, Harmondsworth: Penguin (1978)

Gerard, P. and E. Magnon, *Cartulaire des Templier de Douzens*, Paris: Bibliotheque Nationale (1965)

Gilmour-Bryson, A. (ed. & trans.), *The Trial of the Templars in Cyprus*, Leiden: Brill (1998)

Gilmour-Bryson (ed.), *The Trial of the Templars in the Papal States and the Abruzzi*, Vatican City: Biblioteca Vaticana (1984)

Hemingburgh, Walter of, *Chronicon Domum Walteri de Hemingburgh*, ed. H.C. Hamilton, Rolls Series 82, HMSO (1865)

Household Book of Dame Alice Byrene, 1412–1413, Suffolk Institute of Archaeology and Natural History, 2 (1931)

Joinville, J., *The History of St Louis*, trans N. de Wailly and J. Evans, Oxford: OUP (1938)

Knighton, Henry *Chronica*, ed. J.R. Lumley, HMSO (1963 repr.)

Lees, B. (ed. and trans.), *The Records of the Templars in England in the 12th Century*, British Academy (1935)

Lizerand, G., *Le Dossier de l'affaire des Templiers*, Paris: Librairie Ancienne Honore Champion (1923)

McCoff, D. (ed. and trans.), *The Life of St Mary Magdalene and of her Sister Martha*, Kalamazoo: Cistercian Publications (1989)

Map, William, *De Nugis Curialium*, ed. F.S. Hartland and M.R. James, Cymmorodian Record Series IX (1923)

Michelet, J., *Le Procès des Templiers*, Paris: Les Editions du CTHS (1987)

Obitarium Templi Remensis, Paris: Melanges Historiques, Collection des Documents Inedite (1882)

Paris, Geoffroi de, *La Chronique Metrique attribuée à Geoffroi de Paris*, ed. A. Diverres, Strasbourg: Faculty of Letters of the University of Strasbourg (1957)

Paris, Matthew, *Chronica Majora*, ed. H. Luard, HMSO, Rolls Series 57 (1883)

Paris, Matthew, *Chronicles*, ed. and trans. R. Vaughan, Gloucester: Alan Sutton (1984)

Paris, Matthew, *Flores Historium*, ed. H.R. Luard, HMSO (1890)

Paris, Matthew, *Historia Anglorum*, ed. F. Madden, HMSO (1971 reprint)

Raynaud, G., *Les Gestes des Chiprois*, Geneva: Jules-Guillaume Ficke (1887)

The Register of William Greenfield, Archbishop of York 1306–1315, Surtees Society (1931)

Registrum Clementis Papae V, Rome: Vatican (1887)

Rotuli Literarum Clausum de Turri Londensis, George Eyre (1844)

Rymer, T., *Foedera,* The Hague: Gregg Press (1974 facsimile reprint)

Salisbury, John of, *Historia Pontificalis*, ed. and trans. M. Chibnall (1956)

Sève, R. and A.M. Chagny-Sève, *Le Procès des Templiers d'Auvergne*, Paris: Editions du CTHS (1986)

Stubbs, W. (ed.), *Annales Londondensis*, Rolls series 72, HMSO (1882)

Tyre, William of, *A History of Deeds Done Beyond the Sea*, trans. E. and A.C. Babcock, New York: University of Columbia Press (1948)

Upton-Ward, J. (ed. and trans.), *The Templar Rule*, Woodbridge: Boydell Press (1992)

Wilkins, D., *Concilia Magnae Britannae et Hibernae*, vol. II (1737)

Wilkinson, J. with J. Hill and W. Ryan (eds), *Jerusalem Pilgrimages 1099–1185*, Hakluyt Society, 2nd series, vol. 167 (1988)

Wilson, R. McK., *The Gospel of Philip*, A.R. Mowbray (1962)

Wurzburg, John of, *Descriptiones Terrae Sanctae ex saec*, ed. T. Toble, Leipzig (1956)

Secondary Sources: Books

Addison, G.G., *The History of the Knights Templar*, Longman (2nd ed. 1842)

Andrews, R. and P. Schellenberg, *The Tomb of God*, Little, Brown (1996)

Baigent, M. and R. Leigh, *The Temple and the Lodge*, Arrow Books (1989)

Barber, M. (ed.), *The Military Orders Fighting for the Faith and Caring for the Sick*, Variorum (1994)

Barber, M. *The New Knighthood* , Cambridge: CUP (1994)

Barber, M. *The Trial of the Templars*, Cambridge: CUP (1974)

Blake, P. and P.S. Blezard, *The Arcadian Cipher*, Sidgwick and Jackson (2000)

Boas, A.J., *Jerusalem in the Time of the Crusades*, Routledge (2001)

Bordenove, G., *La Tragedie des Templiers*, Paris: Pygmalion-Gerard Watchet (1993)

Boswell, J., *Christianity, Social Tolerance and Homosexuality*, Chicago: University of Chicago Press (1980)

Brown, D., *The Da Vinci Code*, Corgi (2004)

Burke, P., *Popular Culture in Early Modern Europe*, Wildwood Press (1988)

Burman, E., *Supremely Abominable Crimes: The Trial of the Knights Templar*, Allison and Busby (1994)

Burnes, J., *Sketches of the History of the Temple*, Edinburgh (1844)

Cohn, N., *Europe's Inner Demons*, Pimlico (revised ed. 1993)

Currer-Briggs, N., *The Holy Grail and the Shroud of Christ*, Maulden: ARA Publications (1984)

Demurger, A., *The Last Templar. The Tragedy of Jacques de Molay, Last Grand Master of the Temple* trans. A. Nevill, Profile Books (2004)

Dyer, C., *Standards of hiving in the Middle Ages*, Cambridge: CUP (1990)

Eco, U., *Foucault's Pendulum*, trans. W. Wever, Seckeer & Warburg (1989)

Filson, J., *A New Testament History*, SCM (1964)

Forey, A., *The Fall of the Templars in the Crown of Aragon*, Aldershot: Ashgate (2001)

Garth, H.M., *Saint Mary Magdalene in Medieval Literature* Baltimore: Johns Hopkins University Press (1950)

Green, J., *Rosslyn Chapel. The Enigma and the Myth*, Fort William: Templar Arch Publications (2002)

Haagerman, E. and H. Lincoln, *The Templars Secret Island*, Windrush Press (2000)

Hallam, E., *Chronicles of the Crusades. Eyewitness Accounts of the Wars between Christians and Islam*, Weidenfeld and Nicolson (1989)

Hammer-Purgstall, J., *Die Schuld der Templier*, Vienna: Akad de Wissenschaft (1853)

Janson, K.L., *The Making of the Magdalene*, Princeton NJ: Princeton University Press (1999)

Jolly, K., C. Raudere and E. Peters, *Witchcraft and Magic in Europe. The Middle Ages*, Athlone Press (2002)

Laidler, K., *The Head of God*, Weidenfeld and Nicholson (1998)

Lambert, M., *Medieval Heresy*, Oxford: Blackwell (3rd ed. 2005)

Lea, H.C., *A History of the Inquisition of the Middle Ages*, Sampson Low (1888)

Lea, H.C., *Minor Historical Writings*, Philadelphia: University of Pennsylvania Press (1942)

Levi, E., *The History of Magic*, William Rider and Sons (2nd ed. 1922)

Lincoln, H., *The Holy Place*, Jonathan Cape (1991)

Lock, P., *The Routledge Companion to the Crusades*, Routledge (2006)

Loomis, R.S., *The Grail from Celtic Myth to Christian Symbol*, Cardiff: University of Wales Press (1963)

Lord, E., *The Knights Templar in Britain*, Pearson Education (2004)

Lord, E., *The Stuarts' Secret Army. English Jacobites 1689–1752*, Pearson Education (2004)

Madden, T. (ed.), *The Crusades*, Duncan Baird (2004)

MaiHand, F.W., *Domesday Book and Beyond*, Cambridge: *CUP* (1987)

Martin, E., *The Trial of the Templars*, Allen & Unwin (1928)

Menarche, S., *Clement V*, Cambridge: CUP (1998)

Miguet, M., *Templiers et Hospitallers en Normandie*, Paris: Editions du Comifé de Travaux Historiques er Scientifiques CTHS (1995)

Morris, A.E.J., *History of Urban Form Before the Industrial Revolution*, Longman (3rd ed. 1994)

Morshead, J.G., *The Templar Trials*, Stevens and Son (1888)

Nicholson, H., *The Knights Templar. A New History*, Gloucester: Alan Sutton (2002)

Nicholson, H., *Love, War and the Grail*, Leiden: Brill (2001)

Peters, E., *The Magician, the Witch and the Law*, Philadelphia: University of Pennsylvania Press (1978)

Phillips, G., *The Marian Conspiracy*, Sidgwick and Jackson (2000)

Picknett, L., *Mary Magdalene Christianity's Hidden Goddess*, Robinson (2003)

Porter, R., *Enlightenment*, Harmondsworth: Penguin Books

Prutz, J., *Entwicklung und Untergang des Templeorden* berlin: G. Groesch Verlagbuch (1888)

Richard, J.P., *The Crusades c.1071–c.1291*, Cambridge: CUP (1999)

Riley-Smith, J., *What Were the Crusades*, Macmillan (1977)

Robinson, J., *Born in Blood. The Last Secrets of Freemasonry*, Century Books (1989)

Rosener, W., *Peasants in the Middle Ages*, Oxford: Polity Press (1992)

Scaglione, A., *Knights at Court*, Berkeley: University of California Press (1991)

Schein, S., *Fidelis Crucis. The Papacy, the West and the Recovery of the Holy Land*, Oxford: Clarendon Press (1991)

Selwood, D., *Knights of the Cloister. Templars and Hospitallers in Central-Southern Occitan c.1100–c.1300*, Woodbridge: Boydell Press (1999)

Shahar, S., *The Fourth Estate. A History of Women in the Middle Ages*, Cambridge: CUP (1992)

Strachan, S., *The Mystery of Rosslyn Chapel*, S. Strachan (1996)

Strayer, J.R., *The Reign of Philip the Fair*, Princeton NJ: Princeton University Press (1980)

The Military-Religious Orders: Their History and Continuing Relevance, A record of the meeting convened at Emmanuel College, Cambridge on 17 March 2005

Waite, A.E., *The Holy Grail. Its Legend and Symbolism,* Rider and Co (1933)

Wallace-Murphy, T. and M. Hopkins, *Rosslyn Guardian of the Secrets of the Grail,* Shaftesbury: Element Books Ltd. (1999)

Wilson, G.W., *Photographs of Scottish Scenery: Edinburgh and Roslin*, Edinburgh: William Ritchie (1892)

Wilson, I., *The Blood and the Shroud*, Weidenfeld and Nicholson (1998)

Wilson, I., *The Turin Shroud*, Harmondsworth: Penguin (1979)

Wright, J.R., *The Church and the English Crown 1305–1334*, Toronto: Pontifical Institute of Medieval Studies (1980)

Secondary Sources: Articles

Barber, M., 'Propaganda in the Middle Ages: Charges Against the Templars', *Nottingham Medieval Studies*, vol. XVII (1973)

Barber, M., 'The Turin Shroud' in M. Barber, *Crusaders and Heretics in the 12th–14th Centuries*, Variorum (1995)

Clements, R., 'The Cult of Mary Magdalene in Late Medieval France' in T. Head, (ed.), *Medieval Hagiography*, Garland Publishing (2000)

Divenes, A., 'The grail and the Third Crusade: Thoughts on Le Conte de Grael by Chrétien de Troyes', *Arthurian Literature*, vol. X (1990)

Faireau-Lilee, M.L., 'The Military Orders and the escape of the Christian population from the Holy Land', *Journal of Medieval History*, vol. 19, no. 3, pp. 201–28 (1993)

Forey, A., 'Letters of the Last Two Templar Masters' *Nottingham Medieval Studies*, vol. XLV (2001), pp. 145–71

Fosbrooke, T.H., 'Rothley: the Preceptory', Leicestershire Archaeological Society, *Transactions* (1921–2), pp. 2–32

Gilmor-Bryson, A., 'Sodomy and the Knights Templar', *Journal of the History of Sexuality* vol. 7, no. 2 (1996), pp. 151–83

Hill, R., 'Fourpenny Retirement: The Yorkshire Templars in the Fourteenth Century' in W.J. Sheils and D. Wood (eds), *The Church and Wealth*, Studies in Church History Oxford: Blackwell, (1987) 24

Lord, E., 'The Knights Templar in Hertfordshire: Farmers and Landlords' *Herts Past and Present*, 3rd series, issue 6 (Autumn 2005), pp. 3–11

Menarch, S., 'The Templar Order: A Failed Ideal?' *Catholic Historical Review*, vol. LXXIX (1993)

Riley-Smith, J., 'Were the Templars Guilty?' in S. Ridgard (ed.), *The Medieval Crusade*, Woodbridge: Boydell Press (2004)

Shallow, Justice alias J.G. Morshead, Conjectures on the Templars' Process, Unpublished MS, Cambridge University Library (1918)

Wilkins, G.R. 'The Dissolution of the Templar Ideal in Sir Gawain and the Green Knight', *English Studies*, 63 (1982)

Index